1610-1688

by
J.C. BECKETT

Pretani Press

First published 1990, **Pretani Press**
638 Springfield Road, Belfast BT12 7DY

*This book has received financial assistance under the
Cultural Traditions Programme which aims to encourage
acceptance and understanding of cultural diversity.*

Acknowledgements:
National Portrait Gallery, London
National Library of Ireland for permission to
reproduce "Cromwell's Troops in Wexford 1649"

Cover illustration:
Portrait of James Butler 1st Duke of Ormond
by Sir Peter Lely (NPG 370)

A Nosmada Book

Typeset by Island Publications, Belfast
Printed in N. Ireland by The Universities Press, Belfast

The Cavalier Duke

Contents

PREFACE

Since there are already two biographies of James Butler, first Duke of Ormond, it may seem unnecessary to publish a third. But these earlier works are so long and detailed that they are unlikely to be read save by those with a special interest in the history of the seventeenth century. My own study of Ormond, extending over a period of forty years, has convinced me that he ought to be more widely known than he is; and so I have devoted some of the leisure provided by retirement to writing this brief life in the hope that it would appeal to a wider public. The title I have given it was suggested by Lord Macaulay's description of Ormond, in the ninth chapter of his *History of England*, as 'the most illustrious Cavalier of the great civil war'. Though there may have been others with an equally good claim to be so described, there was no one who maintained more consistently than Ormond the Cavalier principle of loyalty to Church and King.

It should be noted that in the seventeenth century the spelling of names was not so firmly settled as it has since become. In the documents of the period we find both 'Ormond' and 'Ormonde'; the duke himself sometimes used one and sometimes the other in signing his name. I have preferred, unlike earlier biographers of the duke, to use the shorter form.

Finally, I must, as on several earlier occasions, express my gratitude to Mr J.L. Lord: without his encouragement it is unlikely that this book would ever have been completed.

J. C. Beckett

CHAPTER 1

'Jemmy Butler of Kilcash'

(1)

The town of Carrick, on the borders of Tipperary and Waterford, is small, grey and unpretentious; but it is saved from the drabness characteristic of so many Irish country towns by the River Suir, on which it stands, and by its Elizabethan castle. From the twelfth century to the seventeenth Carrick was a principal seat of the powerful Butler family, to whom it owed its prosperity; and it was in Carrick Castle, which he had himself built, that 'Black Tom' Butler, the tenth Earl of Ormond, gathered a large body of his relations and dependants, in December 1613, to celebrate what proved to be the last Christmas of his long and strenuous life. Old and blind, he sat at table in the great hall, wearing, as he always did, even in bed, the blue ribbon of the Garter. Behind his chair, a fair-haired little boy, regardless of the dignified company around him, was busily whipping his top. Puzzled by the noise, Black Tom asked the servant who stood by him what it might be. 'It's young Jemmy Butler a-whipping his gig', said the servant. 'And what Jemmy Butler is that?' asked the earl, for 'James' was one of the commonest of Butler names. 'It's Jemmy Butler of Kilcash', came the servant's reply.

Upon this, the earl demanded that the boy should be brought forward. He placed him between his knees, stroked his head, and fetching a deep sigh said solemnly, 'My house shall be much oppressed and brought very low; but by this boy it shall be restored again, and in his time be in greater splendour than ever it has been.'

Among those who overheard these words was Black Tom's son-in-law, Theobald Butler, who was also his nephew and heir to the earldom. A proud, ill-tempered man, he took the prophecy as an insult to himself, pushed back his chair and flung noisily from the table. But the earl, when told what his son-in-law had done, dismissed him as 'a flower that will soon fade', and added, 'What I have said I am confident will prove true.' And so indeed it did. 'Young Jemmy Butler of Kilcash' became, in time, twelfth Earl and first Duke of

1

Ormond, thrice lord lieutenant of Ireland and, for almost half a century, one of the most influential subjects of the Crown.

Such stories about prophecies of future greatness are always to be regarded with suspicion; and this particular story, which does not seem to have been set down on paper until towards the close of the seventeenth century, is no exception to the rule. Yet there is nothing inherently improbable about it. Black Tom had a poor opinion of his son-in-law and he had an old man's affection for the child whose glory he foretold, and whose chance of succeeding to the Ormond title was not, even in 1613, so remote as to make the prophecy appear absurd. Theobald Butler was still childless, after ten years of married life; and if he were to die without male issue Jemmy Butler of Kilcash would come into the direct line of succession. Not was it unnatural that the old earl should foresee a period of trouble and distress for his family. Since he had no legitimate son to succeed him the title would pass, after his death, to his nephew. But what of his only daughter's claim to his landed estates? If these had to be divided, his daughter's share might well pass out of Butler hands; and both the wealth and influence of the new head of the family would be irreparably damaged. It was to avert this catastrophe that the match between his daughter and Theobald had been arranged, but so far it had produced no heir; and until this happened the future would remain uncertain. Black Tom had lost the sight of his eyes, but his mental vision was still sharp; he may well have foreseen, in general terms, the troubles that did, in fact, beset his family after his death and reduce it, for a time, to poverty and helplessness. And a combination of hope and affection might easily make him regard the little boy of whom he was so fond as the destined restorer of the Butler fortunes.

(2)

The Butlers had been settled in Ireland since the twelfth century, having followed not long after those hardy Anglo-Norman adventurers whom the king of Leinster, Dermot MacMurrough, had called in to fight his battles against his numerous enemies. This action of his produced results that no one had foreseen. Hitherto, English kings had hardly troubled themselves about Ireland, a country lying outside the orbit of European politics, divided into warring kingdoms and living, it was generally supposed, in a kind of semi-heathen darkness.

But Henry II could not stand aside and allow a group of his subjects to establish an independent Anglo-Norman power just across the Irish Sea and in dangerous proximity to Wales. He followed them to Ireland with an army, not to conquer the country, but to keep these dangerous subjects of his in order. He met no opposition from anyone. Not only the Anglo-Norman leaders but the Gaelic kings as well readily submitted to his authority; and to give formal expression to the new state of affairs Henry assumed the title, conferred on him by the pope some years earlier, of 'Lord of Ireland'. He neither planned nor attempted any conquest of the country; but for the next century and more the Anglo-Normans already in Ireland, and others who followed after them, gradually extended the area under their control, at the expense of the Gaelic monarchies.

It was while this process of expansion was in its early stages that the first of the Butlers, Theobald, established himself in Ireland. He was the first in a quite literal sense, for it was from his hereditary office of 'Botiller', or cup-bearer, to the Lord of Ireland that the family derived its patronymic. About the family's earlier history not much is known with certainty. But pride of family is rarely willing to be confined by the rules of evidence; and the Butlers long claimed to include among their forebears not only Richard the Good, duke of Normandy, but also Agnes Becket, sister to the 'holy blissful martyr', Thomas of Canterbury. Such claims, however ill-founded they might be, are not altogether without significance; for they indicated a continuing consciousness of association with a larger world than that of Ireland. Many of the Anglo-Norman families that settled there during the twelfth and thirteenth centuries learned, by degrees, to copy the habits of their Gaelic neighbours; and some became, in the old phrase, 'more Irish than the Irish themselves'. But the Butlers showed little tendency to move in this direction. As their estates expanded they endowed religious houses, built castles, encouraged the growth of towns, promoted trade - in short, they sought to establish and maintain the social and economic order with which they, or their ancestors, had been familiar in England and in Normandy.

It would be misleading to suppose that the Butlers, and other Anglo-Norman and English settlers who tried to maintain their own traditions, were on that account less than genuinely Irish. Gaelic they were not; yet they were acting in very much the same way as the Gaels had acted before them. For the Gaels, too, were invaders, who had subdued and dispossessed the earlier inhabitants; and they, too,

3

had maintained, in the land they had conquered, the language and customs they had brought with them. And just as the Gaels, for all their conservatism, were moulded by the conditions of life in Ireland, so too the Anglo-Normans, however tenacious of their old traditions, were gradually transformed. They might insist that they were English, but they were English with a difference. They were 'the English of Ireland', an integral part of Irish life, which, as it developed through the succeeding centuries, has been quite as strongly marked by their influence as by that of their Gaelic predecessors.

During the thirteenth century and the early decades of the fourteenth Butler power expanded with the general expansion of Anglo-Norman influence; and they came, in time, to dominate the greater part of the counties of Kilkenny and Tipperary. They rose in rank also: in 1315 Edmund, fifth in succession from Theobald, was raised to the peerage as Earl of Carrick; and a little more than ten years later his son and successor James, the first of the name, was created Earl of Ormond. From this time onwards the Carrick title, despite its precedence in time, fell into disuse, perhaps because Ormond (that is, North Munster) conveyed a stronger impression of territorial power than Carrick, which was the name of a single manor. But when the earldom of Ormond was created the Anglo-Norman power had ceased to expand and very soon Gaelic kings began to recover, by degrees, much of the territory they had lost. The English monarchy, distracted by foreign and domestic troubles, was in no position to send reinforcements; and it seemed as if it was doomed to lose the Lordship of Ireland, not as the result of any concerted rebellion, for nothing of the sort occurred, but simply by the gradual collapse of such central authority as still survived.

In these conditions, the tendency of Anglo-Norman families to forget their origins and adopt a Gaelic way of life became more strongly marked than ever. This was a tendency that the Butlers continued to resist steadily. They maintained their traditional place among 'the English of Ireland'; and they strengthened the tradition by making, from time to time, marriage alliances with the English of England. One such alliance was of some significance for the future. In the 1470s Margaret, daughter of Thomas, seventh Earl of Ormond, married Sir William Boleyn, and thus became grandmother of Anne Boleyn, Henry VIII's second wife. The connection was not altogether forgotten; and the favour that Anne Boleyn's daughter, Queen

4

Elizabeth, constantly showed to Black Tom Butler almost certainly owed something to her recognition of the kinship between them.

The Ireland over which Queen Elizabeth ruled was very different from what it had been in the days of her Irish great-grandmother. In the early decades of the sixteenth century the English monarchy, alarmed at the attempts of its continental enemies to establish a base in Ireland, had at last begun to assert itself. The Dublin administration, instead of being left to go its own way, was brought under direct and continuous English control; and Anglo-Norman and Gaelic rulers were forced, by degrees, to recognize that it was now an effective centre of power. In 1541 Henry VIII signalized the monarchy's new attitude by proclaiming himself 'King of Ireland' - a natural enough move on his part, since the earlier title, 'Lord of Ireland', rested on papal authority, which he had now renounced. To outward appearance, Henry's policy went well: no one objected to his new title; and papal authority found few champions among either clergy or laity. But the appearance proved deceptive. Local rulers, Anglo-Norman and Gaelic, were ready enough to do homage, swear allegiance and recognize the king as head of the church; but they resented any restriction on their freedom to make war on their neighbours. When it became clear, in the reigns of Edward VI and Elizabeth, that royal supremacy in the church brought with it the Protestant Reformation, this resentment found a religious sanction. A new and enduring source of conflict had entered into Irish life.

This is not to say that the Irish war of Elizabeth's reign was primarily a war of religion. It was, in essence, a typical sixteenth-century struggle between a centralizing government and local rulers determined to retain the practical independence to which they and their ancestors had been accustomed. Even if the Protestant Reformation had never occurred, such a war would have had to be fought before Ireland could be brought under a single effective administration. It was natural, then, that the crown should have the support of those who, from loyalty or interest, wished to see its authority firmly established, even though they disagreed with its ecclesiastical policy. Such people formed a powerful element among 'the English of Ireland'; and without their help the decisive victory that Elizabeth's forces finally achieved, in the last months of her reign, could hardly have been won.

During this troubled period the fortunes of the Butler family were guided by Black Tom, who in 1546 had succeeded his father, the ninth Earl of Ormond, at the age of fourteen. He spent the next eight years at the English court; and it was not until 1554 that he came to Ireland to take over the management of his estates. His English upbringing had made him a protestant, the first, and for long the only, protestant in the family. But his faith, though he retained it throughout life, was neither bigoted nor aggressive. In political matters, also, he was equally inclined to moderation. Though perfectly loyal to the crown, he had little sympathy with the uncompromising attitude displayed by many English commanders in Ireland; and he advocated a more conciliatory policy: 'The queen hath many good subjects here' he wrote in 1570, 'if they were but cherished and not overpressed'. But when fighting became necessary he was never backward: his skill and courage made an invaluable contribution to the establishment and maintenance of royal authority in Munster. Naturally enough, he had an eye to the interests of his family; but he did not seek to build up its fortunes on the ruin of others and repeatedly used his influence with the queen to obtain pardon for defeated rebels. His character emerges as that of a protestant without bigotry, a commander courageous in the field and moderate in victory, an Irishman who combined loyalty to the crown with constant concern about his country and his countrymen. Such was Black Tom Butler, whom his great-great-nephew, the twelfth Earl of Ormond, was to regard as the man who, of all his predecessors in the title, was most worthy of admiration.

(3)

Theobald Butler, to whom Black Tom had married his only daughter, Elizabeth, died, still childless, before his father-in-law; and in the history of the Butler family his death is much more significant than any action he performed in his lifetime. In the first place, it revived the possibility, which his marriage had been meant to avert, of a legal dispute over the inheritance of the Ormond estates. In the second place, it meant that the heir to the earldom was now another of Black Tom's nephews, Sir Walter Butler of Kilcash - known, on account of his piety, as 'Walter of the beads and rosary'; and Sir Walter was the grandfather of that Jemmy Butler whose future greatness Black Tom had foretold.

Some five years before Theobald's death Sir Walter's son and heir, Thomas, had married Elizabeth Poyntz, of a wealthy recusant family in Gloucestershire. He could not bring his bride to Kilcash, for Sir Walter disapproved of the marriage; and for a time the couple lived in London, with the lady's father, Sir John Poyntz, at Clerkenwell. And here, on 19 October 1610, their eldest son, James, was born. Not long afterwards the parents removed to Ireland, where, though Kilcash was still closed to them, they were befriended by Black Tom. James, however, was left behind in London, to be nursed by a carpenter's wife at Hatfield; and it was not until 1613 that he was brought over to Ireland. To the end of his life he remembered the excitement of that journey; and he remembered also the kindness with which he was received by the old blind earl at Carrick, where he and his parents were frequent guests. But Black Tom's long life was now near its end; and on his death, in November 1614, Sir Walter succeeded him as the eleventh Earl of Ormond; and James's father became, by courtesy, the Viscount Thurles.

His accession to the earldom brought Sir Walter little but anxiety and distress, for the long-feared dispute over the inheritance of the Ormond estates broke out almost at once. After Theobald's death Elizabeth Butler had not been allowed to remain long a widow. King James seized the opportunity to provide for one of his numerous Scottish dependants; and on his insistence she was married to Sir Richard Preston, whom he raised to the peerage as Lord Dingwall. Black Tom's death occurred only a few months after this marriage; and Lord Dingwall lost little time in putting forward his wife's claim as heir general to his estates. How the case might have gone had it been left to the ordinary course of law it is impossible to be sure. But King James was unwilling to take chances; and he induced both contestants to submit the matter to his arbitration, binding themselves, under heavy financial penalties, to accept his decision. Dingwall, of course, could agree to this arrangement with an easy mind. Earl Walter probably regarded it as the lesser of two evils; for it had already become clear that the judges were likely to be influenced quite as much by the king's known wishes as by the evidence before them.

James took his time over the case and made a decent show of considering both sides. But his judgement, when it came, was a shock to the earl; the Ormond estates were to be divided and a good half, including the castle of Kilkenny with all its valuable contents, was to go to Lord Dingwall in right of his wife. Even the king seems to have thought that his countryman had been generously treated; but he thought, also, that a nobleman with such extensive estates in Ireland should have an Irish title and created him, not long afterwards, Earl of Desmond.

Walter Butler's fate was very different. Indignant at what he regarded as gross injustice, he flatly refused either to accept the king's decision or to pay the enormous fine to which, in the event of such refusal, he had bound himself. To bring him to a more compliant frame of mind the king lodged him in the Fleet prison; and here, for the next six years, he subsisted meagrely on the charity of an old servant; for the rents even of the lands due to him by the king's award were now all sequestered by the crown.

While his grandfather lay in prison James Butler, also, had fallen into the king's hands, though after a rather different fashion. In December 1619 his father had been drowned off the coast of County Dublin, in the course of a voyage from Ireland to England; and James, at nine years of age, became Viscount Thurles and the immediate heir to the earldom.[1] Here again King James saw an opportunity of which he might make use. If the young viscount could be shown to be a ward of the crown he could be brought up as a protestant, which would not only be to his own spiritual advantage but would serve to promote the protestant cause in Ireland. The claim to wardship was, at best, dubious; but the crown lawyers showed their customary ingenuity and James, Viscount Thurles, was declared to be the king's ward. In the meantime, his mother had placed him with a Roman Catholic tutor at Finchley; but now, by the king's orders, he was transferred to Lambeth and placed under the care of George Abbot, archbishop of Canterbury.

He can hardly have found the next few years very happy. The king neglected his maintenance, allowing only forty pounds a years to meet all his expenses; and the archbishop neglected his education, so that at the end of five years he was still ignorant of Latin, at a time when Latin was regarded as an essential key to knowledge. Yet the period under Abbot's tutelage had a lasting effect upon the whole course of his life; for it was during this period that he became a protestant. Outward conformity to the Church of England he could not, in the circumstances, have avoided; and such conformity would probably have been enough to satisfy the archbishop; but Lord Thurles

1. Lady Thurles subsequently married George Mathew, by whom she had a second family. During the Restoration period one of her sons by this marriage, George, managed the estates of his half-brother, the Duke of Ormond.

became, though under whose influence we do not know, a convinced as well as a conforming protestant, and one well able to defend his faith in argument. The loyalty to the crown that marked his whole career was part of the Butler tradition; but his even stronger devotion to the established church must be traced to the years he passed at Lambeth.

(4)

All this time Earl Walter lay in prison, while his wife and daughters, reduced to poverty, lived as best they could. At last, worn out by suffering, he gave up the hopeless struggle and submitted to the crown. In 1625 he recovered his liberty and the portion of the Ormond estates that King James's judgement had left him. For some years, however, he remained in London; and he eventually obtained, though not without difficulty, permission for his grandson and heir to live with him at his house in Drury Lane.

Now, for the first time, the young Lord Thurles had the opportunity and means to live the life appropriate to his age and rank. He frequented the court and the theatres; and he displayed his martial ardour by dashing off to Portsmouth, in August 1628, to enlist as a volunteer in Buckingham's expedition to Rochelle. The duke, though a patron of Lord Desmond and no friend to the Butlers, received him kindly; but when he found that the young man had left London without the consent or knowledge of his grandfather he sent him home again. This was a disappointment to Lord Thurles; but he soon had another and more important matter to think of - marriage.

The Earl and Countess of Desmond had only one child, the Lady Elizabeth Preston; and if she were to marry the heir to the earldom of Ormond the two halves of the estate would be re-united. It was not a new idea: such a marriage had been projected as early as 1620, when Elizabeth was barely five years old; but at that time the families had failed to agree upon terms. And soon there was another suitor in the field, George Fielding, a nephew of the Duke of Buckingham, who used all his influence to promote the match. Though the Countess of Desmond herself was still well-disposed towards a Butler alliance, her husband was not the man to oppose the wishes of the king's all-powerful favourite; and the matter seemed as good as settled. But the situation changed with dramatic suddenness. In August 1628 Buckingham was assassinated, on the eve of his departure for Rochelle.

In October of the same year the Earl of Desmond was drowned in the Irish Sea. Just three weeks earlier his countess had died, urging upon her daughter, almost with her last breath, the duty of marrying the heir to the Ormond earldom. At long last Earl Walter could see some hope that the family fortunes, which had been so heavily damaged by one marriage alliance, might be restored by another.

There was still, however, a formidable obstacle to be overcome. King Charles had granted the wardship of Elizabeth Preston to Lord Holland; and he, close-fisted and ambitious, would certainly try to keep such a wealthy heiress for one of his own connection. But the king, perhaps from an uneasy feeling that the Butlers had been hardly treated, now favoured their cause; Lord Holland, after months of opposition, allowed himself to be bought off; and in December 1629, little more than a year after she had lost her parents, the Lady Elizabeth Preston was married to James, Lord Thurles, heir apparent to the earldom of Ormond. The bride was fourteen and a half years old; the bridegroom had just turned nineteen.

To all appearance, this was a marriage of convenience, dictated solely by family interests; and the business character of the transaction was emphasized by the fact that Lord Holland demanded and received £15,000 in return for his consent to the match. Yet the union proved a remarkably happy one; and even in the steps that led up to it the element of romance was not altogether lacking. We need not accept the story, dating from many years later, that Lord Thurles, having contrived to sit beside the Lady Elizabeth in church, later visited Holland House, which was otherwise closed to him, in the disguise of a pedlar and passed her a letter concealed in a pair of gloves, to which she, with precocious ingenuity, managed to send a reply. Carte's statement that the couple met and conversed at court is more probable, if also more prosaic. But there was certainly some understanding between them, independent of the negotiations carried on by their elders; and they maintained a private correspondence. This was made possible through the co-operation of one of Lord Holland's daughters, Lady Isabella Rich, who had already developed that love of intrigue for which, after her marriage to Sir James Thynne, she was to become so celebrated.

On this occasion, at least, Lady Isabella allowed her feelings to outrun her discretion. In her capacity as go-between she was obliged to have, from time to time, confidential meetings with Lord Thurles in places where they were secure from interruption. It was a dangerous proceeding. She was lively; he was handsome; both were young. It is hardly surprising that mutual attraction led them to forget, for a time, the business they had in hand; and Lady Isabella found herself with child by her friend's lover. She managed to conceal her condition until she was safely delivered of a son, who was quickly smuggled abroad; and no one in either family seems to have known anything of the episode. More than twenty years later the Lady Elizabeth, now Marchioness of Ormond, stumbled upon the secret by accident; and it is pleasant to be able to record that she showed no resentment and that the friendship between the two ladies survived the disclosure.

We know little of James Butler's doings in the years immediately after his marriage. Indeed, personal records of his early life are very scanty; and they consist, for the most part, of recollections - both his own and those of others - not written down until much later. It is clear, however, that he was active, of a cheerful disposition and fond of company; and there are indications also of the strong sense of duty that was to be the outstanding characteristic of his later life. But in his youth he certainly showed an impulsiveness and a love of change of which there is little sign later on. A few days after the wedding he took his bride into Gloucestershire, on a long visit to his maternal uncle, Sir John Poyntz, at Acton; and here he tried to remedy some of the defects in his education by studying Latin with his chaplain. A year later he moved to Carrick, where Earl Walter had now settled down. Probably he found life with his elderly grandparents and his child wife dull enough. At any rate, he did not stay at Carrick long. Within twelve months he set off for Scotland, by himself, to visit his wife's relations there. From Scotland he went to London, on business connected with the estate; and in London he remained, on business or pleasure, for almost two years. But when he did set off for home, in the summer of 1633, he wasted no time on the journey. At four o'clock on a Saturday morning he left London; by nine o'clock next evening he was on board the *Ninth Whelp* in Bristol harbour; and he sat down to dinner in Carrick Castle at three o'clock on Monday afternoon.[1] But things had changed since he had last eaten there; for his grandfather had died in February, and he had now entered into his

---

1. The precise date of this journey is doubtful. Carte places it in September; but this is clearly wrong, for Ormond was certainly in Dublin on 24 July, when he had an interview with the lord deputy, Sir Thomas Wentworth. Carte himself states that Ormond arrived in Dublin before Wentworth, who landed there on 23 July.

inheritance. Jemmy Butler of Kilcash was now James, twelfth Earl of Ormond and one of the wealthiest and most powerful of Irish noblemen.

CHAPTER II

Apprenticeship

(1)

Ormond's return to Ireland in 1633 marked the opening of a new era in his life. He had entered into his inheritance; and he readily accepted the responsibilities as well as the privileges that it brought with it. He was almost twenty-three years of age, a little above average height, very strongly made and capable of great endurance - a year or so earlier he had ridden in three days from Edinburgh to Ware, a distance of four hundred miles, without feeling any fatigue. Though his early education had been neglected, he had done what he could to remedy this defect; and his letters and dispatches are written in a clear and vigorous style that reflects the character of the writer.[1] He was proud of his rank and lineage, but never arrogant; and though at this early stage of his career he could sometimes act impulsively, experience soon taught him patience and restraint.

Ireland had at this time enjoyed an unusually long period of peace: in 1630 the Earl of Cork, with forty years' experience of Irish life, declared that he had never known the country so quiet. But, despite this appearance of calm, Irish society was deeply and dangerously divided. The majority of the population - commonly described by English contemporaries as 'the Irish', 'the native Irish' or 'the Old Irish' - was of Gaelic or pre-Gaelic origin. But from the twelfth century onwards there had been an influx of Anglo-Norman and English settlers; and it was their descendants who now dominated the economic and political life of the country. Since the latter half of the sixteenth century the situation had been complicated by a difference in ecclesiastical allegiance. Early in Elizabeth's reign the Irish parliament, under pressure from the crown, had passed acts of

1. Bishop Burnet, who was a younger contemporary of Ormond, declared that 'he writes the best of any man that has no learning, that I ever knew'. In saying that Ormond had 'no learning' Burnet meant that he had not had a university education.

supremacy and uniformity essentially the same as those passed in England; and the ecclesiastical establishment had been reorganized on the English model. But the bulk of the population had refused to conform; and the adherents of the established church consisted mainly, though not exclusively, of newly-arrived settlers - the 'New English', as they were commonly called, to distinguish them from the 'Old English', whose families had been settled in Ireland for generations.

In the past both Old Irish and Old English had often been in revolt against the crown; and though at this time the country had been at peace for almost a generation, no government could feel itself secure without a standing army, the cost of which was the heaviest charge upon the revenue. But in the early 1630s the revenue had, for various reasons, declined; and the army was in consequence ill-paid and ill-equipped. When Thomas Wentworth - later Earl of Strafford - was sworn in as lord deputy,[1] in July 1633, he at once set himself to reform the army; and it was Ormond's ready assistance in the task that brought the two men together.

Wentworth's first business was to raise money. Some years earlier the nobility and gentry had agreed to pay a voluntary contribution towards the upkeep of the army in return for certain concessions by the crown; but these payments had now ceased, and Wentworth opened negotiations for their renewal. In this Ormond gave such effective support that in June 1634 Wentworth sent him a letter of thanks, commending his zeal in the king's service. Though the letter is for the most part formal, one sentence in it suggests that the two were already on fairly intimate terms: 'I desire my service may be presented to your noble lady, and I beseech God make you happy in a young son'. Wentworth clearly knew that Lady Ormond was with child; and a few weeks later his prayer was fulfilled when she gave birth to a son, who was christened Thomas, after 'Black Tom', the tenth earl. He was her second son, but the first - also christened Thomas - had died at two days old. This Thomas, who later became Earl of Ossory, was to survive into manhood and to win fame by his exploits both at sea and on land in the reign of Charles II.

Little more than a week after the birth of his son Ormond came near to losing the lord deputy's favour. Wentworth had received the

1. When the lord lieutenant was absent, or when there was no lord lieutenant, the crown was represented either by a lord deputy or by lords justices, usually two in number, but occasionally three. Sometimes, but rarely, the government was entrusted to a single lord justice.

king's permission to summon a parliament, which was formally opened on 14 July 1634. Next day the houses met for the transaction of business; and Wentworth, fearing that disputes between members might lead to actual violence - as had, indeed, nearly happened in the house of commons some twenty years earlier - issued an order requiring both lords and commons to surrender their swords before entering their respective chambers. To this everyone submitted, except Ormond. He refused to hand over his sword; and when the usher of the black rod, having shown him the deputy's order, renewed his request, Ormond told him brusquely that if he had his sword it should be in his guts, entered the house and took his place.

Wentworth was not a man to tolerate such a challenge to his authority; and before the day was over Ormond had been summoned before the council to answer for his conduct. He defended himself on the grounds that, though the lord deputy had bidden him surrender his sword, a higher authority had bidden him wear it. In justification, he produced his summons to parliament, which ran in the king's name, and instructed him to appear *cum gladio cintus* - girt with a sword.[1] Wentworth, though he felt obliged to accept this defence, was at first inclined to resent what he regarded as a slight to his own authority. But he quickly decided that it would be foolish to alienate one who had already shown himself zealous in the king's service. In the task that lay before him he would need all the help he could get; and Ormond, with his rank, his wealth and his wide family connections, would be a useful ally. Instead, therefore, of allowing this incident to break the friendly relationship he had already formed with Ormond, he did his best to strengthen it. Some months later, in a report to Sir John Coke, one of the king's secretaries of state, he spoke very highly of Ormond, declaring that among the members of the house of lords he had 'as much advantage of the rest in judgement and parts, as he hath in estate and blood'. He recommended that he should be made a member of the council, despite his comparative youth: 'he is young, but take it from me, a very staid head'. This advice was followed: in January 1635 Ormond became a privy councillor; and during the next half-dozen years he was one of Wentworth's most loyal and effective supporters.

1. The episode was recounted, many years later, by Ormond himself to Sir Robert Southwell, one of his closest friends, who had undertaken to write his biography. Though Southwell never completed this work, the material he had collected was used by Thomas Carte.

It was, then, under Wentworth's leadership that Ormond entered on his long career of service to the crown; and when, a few years later, Wentworth fell from power and his policy came under attack both in Ireland and in England, Ormond refused to join with the majority. But, despite their close association, the two men were very different in character and outlook. Wentworth was authoritarian; he enjoyed the exercise of power and resented any show of opposition as if it were an insult to himself. Ormond, though he would never abandon his principles, was prepared to listen to an opponent and to go as far as his conscience would allow him in seeking agreement. In the troubled times that lay ahead his readiness to negotiate and his patience in seeking a settlement acceptable to both sides did much to postpone, though they could not in the end avert, the collapse of the royalist cause in Ireland.

(2)

Both as a councillor and as a member of the house of lords Ormond acquired some useful experience of political affairs. But his duties as an army officer took up more of his time than either council or parliament. He came of a family with a long tradition of military service; and shortly after he settled at Carrick in 1633, he acquired, by purchase, command of a troop of carabins - mounted musketeers. Unlike many Irish officers of the period he took his duties seriously; and in 1638 Wentworth added to his responsibilities by appointing him commander of a troop of cuirassiers. Two years later, in a period of great complexity and danger, he was to be entrusted with the command of the whole Irish army.

The crisis that was to bring him such rapid promotion had its origin on the other side of the Irish Sea. While royal authority had been growing stronger in Ireland under Wentworth's stern government it was being openly defied in Scotland. Charles's attempt to bring the Scottish church into conformity with the English had aroused widespread opposition, expressed in a National Covenant drawn up in February 1638; and it was clear that the Scots were prepared to fight rather than yield. Charles, determined to compel obedience, set about raising an army to invade Scotland. His first attempt, in the early summer of 1639, collapsed without a shot being fired on either side; and the treaty of Berwick (18 June) left things very much as they were. The king, who had no thought of abandoning his policy, now conceived the idea of using Irish troops to enforce his policy in Scotland. He sent for Wentworth, who arrived in London in September; and from then until his impeachment in November 1640 he was the king's most trusted adviser. Together they planned to raise a new Irish army of 8,000 foot and 1,000 horse, to be available for service wherever the king might require it; and in March 1640 Wentworth - now Earl of Strafford and with the more prestigious rank of lord lieutenant, instead of, as before, lord deputy - returned to Ireland to give effect to these decisions.

Strafford landed at Dublin on 18 March and at once set about his task. To outward appearance, at least. his success was complete. Parliament readily voted the funds for which he asked; and the recruitment of men for the new army was soon in progress. Barely a fortnight later he was on his way back to England, and, as it proved, to imprisonment and execution. Strafford's brief stay in Ireland marked a turning-point in Ormond's career. Up to this time, though he had served the crown well, he had held no post of great importance. Now, in the new army that was being formed, he was not only to be colonel of a cavalry regiment and lieutenant-general of horse but was also to be commander-in-chief during Strafford's absence.

There can be no doubt that the choice of Ormond for this post reflected Strafford's desire to have at the head of the army, during his own absence, a man on whose support he could rely. In practice most of the duty fell on the sergeant-major-general, Sir William St. Leger, an old and experienced soldier, who had served with the Dutch against the Spaniards while Ormond was still a child. It was he who undertook the duty of training the new recruits; and when, in the summer of 1640, the army was ready to march north to Carrickfergus, where it would be within easy reach of Scotland, he was still in command, for Ormond was detained at Kilkenny by the illness of his wife. Lady Ormond was again with child; and though she was safely delivered of a daughter (Elizabeth) at the end of June, she herself remained so ill that for almost a month after the birth Ormond was unwilling to leave her.

Meanwhile the political situation had been changing. When parliament met again in June it showed none of the readiness to support royal policy that it had shown in March. Instead, it proved so critical of the government that the lord deputy, Sir Christopher

17

Wandesford, prorogued it after little more than a fortnight. But when it re-assembled in October it was in an even more aggressive mood; and Strafford's policy was openly attacked in both houses. The commons drew up a long remonstrance, in which almost everything that he had done or attempted to do was condemned; and this remonstrance provided his English enemies with material for many of the charges they brought against him at his impeachment a few months later. An attempt to secure the approval of the house of lords for a similar remonstrance would probably have succeeded but for Ormond's vigorous opposition - a service for which the king sent him a letter of thanks in November 1640.

When this letter was written the Long Parliament had been in session for some weeks; the house of commons had opened its attack upon Strafford; and he was now a prisoner in the Tower, where he remained until his execution on 12 May 1641. Strafford was often ruthless, but he could be grateful to those who had served him well; and one of his last requests to the king was that his place in the order of the Garter should be filled by the appointment of Ormond. It was typical of Ormond's unselfish devotion to the crown that when the offer was made he asked leave to decline it, on the ground that the conferment of such a high honour might serve to attach to the royal cause some nobleman whose support would otherwise be doubtful.

(3)

On 8 May, four days before Strafford's execution, the king had sent Ormond instructions to disband the recently-enlisted Irish army, which was still stationed in the north. There was some difficulty in raising enough money to pay the soldiers even a small part of what was owing to them; but despite this, the task was quickly and peacefully accomplished. By disbanding the army the king no doubt hoped to allay the fears expressed in the house of commons that he intended to use Irish troops to support his authority in England. Whether or not he had any such idea is doubtful; but within a short time he was planning to re-assemble the disbanded army. His principal agent in the business was Randal MacDonnell, Earl of Antrim; and the only coherent account of what was intended is that given by him many years later. According to this account Antrim and Ormond were to re-assemble as many of the troops as they could and then take possession of Dublin castle in the king's name. Antrim was a notorious braggart and liar; and probably the strongest reason for accepting his account as substantially true is that Ormond never, so far as is known, made any comment upon it. He had great reverence for the memory of King Charles I; and if he could not clear him completely from having devised or sanctioned such a scheme he would feel that the only safe course was to maintain silence.

Nothing came of the scheme outlined by Antrim. The attempt to re-assemble the army was soon abandoned; and without the support of an army there was nothing that could be done. But if, as is possible, some hint of what had been intended reached a group of conspirators who also were planning to seize Dublin Castle it may well have encouraged them to proceed.

The leading figure among these conspirators was Rory O'More, whose family, once wealthy and powerful, had now lost most of its property. He was convinced that the native Irish should use the opportunity provided by the quarrel between king and parliament in England to rise in revolt and recover their former possessions. Both he and those who joined with him professed their loyalty to the crown; but they were determined that Ireland should for the future be governed in their own interests and not in those of the English settlers.

By the summer of 1641 their plans were far advanced. The insurrection was to begin in Ulster on 23 October; and on the same day Dublin Castle was to be seized. Though many hundreds of people were of necessity involved in the conspiracy, the secret was so well kept that neither the Ulster protestants nor the government in Dublin had the slightest suspicion of what was being prepared for them. When, on the evening of Friday 22 October, Sir William Parsons, one of the lords justices, received warning of a plot to take possession of Dublin Castle next day he was at first inclined to dismiss it as an idle rumour. He did, however, take the necessary precautions. Dublin Castle was saved. But next day the insurrection in Ulster broke out as planned; and by midnight the first of a long stream of refugees, with frightening tales of slaughter and destruction, had reached Dublin.

CHAPTER III

The King's Man in Ireland: 1641 - 1647

(1)

Between the outbreak of the Ulster insurrection in October 1641 and the end of 1650 the history of Ormond's life is inseparable from the history of Ireland. Directly or indirectly he was involved in all that happened; and in the many-sided conflict that filled the decade his influence was a factor that must always be taken into account. There were others whose achievements were more spectacular or more enduring; but there was no one who was so continuously at the centre of affairs. It was to him that the king turned in October 1641; and it was his departure for exile abroad in December 1650 that marked the final collapse of the royalist cause in Ireland.

At the opening of this troubled decade Ormond was still a comparatively young man, just over thirty-one years of age. His early advancement in the royal service had been due rather to his birth and rank than to anything that was known of his abilities, for Strafford had been anxious to secure the support of a wealthy nobleman and head of a powerful family. As a councillor and, later, as lieutenant-general of the army he had gained some experience of civil and military administration. But he had never taken a leading part in the work of the council; and his ability as a soldier had never been tested in war. There were other men during this critical period who were raised by their native ability from obscurity to eminence. But Ormond's case was different. Had he been born a simple country gentleman he would, no doubt, have done his duty as he saw it; but it is very unlikely that he would have played any prominent part in the shaping of events. The responsibilities he had to bear were part of his inheritance; and in this spirit he accepted them, more concerned to maintain his family's tradition of loyalty to the crown than to gain distinction or advancement for himself.

Though Ormond's outstanding characteristic was his loyalty, this alone would not have made him, over so many years, the mainstay of the royal cause in Ireland. He had other qualities, unspectacular but

21

solid, which were of the greatest service to the king. In face of danger and disappointment he showed an unruffled courage that inspired others to maintain the struggle. He had an obvious honesty of purpose that won the respect and confidence of his troops, though their pay was constantly in arrears and they were sometimes almost starving. In negotiations with the insurgents, undertaken at the king's command, he showed a dogged patience that enabled him to establish a truce on reasonable terms and without any sacrifice of principle. At a later stage, when the king's cause in England lay in ruins, the same patient skill enabled him to build up in Ireland a royalist alliance that might, but for the inveterate divisiveness of the Irish Catholics, have tempered, at least, the catastrophic effect of the Cromwellian onslaught.

Ormond's usefulness to the king depended mainly on his own character and abilities; but in his negotiations with the insurgents he derived great advantage from his birth and rank. By the end of 1641 the Old English recusants had joined forces with the Ulster Irish; and they soon assumed a leading place in directing the insurgents' affairs. Among them were many of Ormond's relations (for he was almost the only protestant in the widespread Butler connection) and many others with whom he had long been on friendly terms. Traditional respect for the head of the Butler family and personal regard for Ormond himself survived even the strain of open war; and once negotiations for peace began, in 1643, he could afford to take a firmer line and impose more rigorous conditions than would have been possible for anyone else. If, in the end, all his efforts brought little material advantage to the king, this was not due to any neglect on his part, but to circumstances, in England as well as in Ireland, that it was beyond his power to control.

In the summer and autumn of 1641 Ormond can have had no idea of the long, hazardous and, at the last, apparently fruitless labour that lay ahead of him. When the parliamentary session ended, in June, he had retired with his wife and children to his house at Carrick, a hundred miles south of Dublin. Here he laid aside politics and busied himself chiefly in trying to secure from the king a restoration of the palatine rights in County Tipperary that his ancestors had enjoyed for centuries. These rights had been confiscated, with little show of justice, by King James as a mark of his displeasure with Earl Walter; and Ormond now hoped to recover them. In October his agent in this affair, Sir Patrick Wemyss, was in Edinburgh, where the king then was, promoting Ormond's claims. It was by Sir Patrick Wemyss that the king, as soon as he had received news of the insurrection in Ulster, sent a letter instructing Ormond to resume his post as lieutenant-general of the army.

(2)

The lords justices, Sir William Parsons and Sir John Borlase, had sent for Ormond as soon as they received news of the insurrection; and he was already in Dublin when Sir Patrick Wemyss arrived there on 10 November. His commission as lieutenant-general had lapsed on the death of Strafford, under whom he held it, and had not been renewed by Strafford's successor as lord lieutenant, the Earl of Leicester. Now, on the king's instructions sent by Wemyss, the lords justices issued a new commission and Ormond resumed command of the army. His first task was to raise more troops. There was no difficulty in finding recruits among the thousands of refugees who had fled from Ulster; Strafford had laid in a plentiful supply of arms; and Ormond soon had at his disposal a force of some four thousand men.

If he had had his way he would at once have taken the offensive against the insurgents, in the hope of crushing them before they had time to collect more arms and improve their organization. But the lords justices rejected this proposal and insisted on a more cautious policy. This decision was no doubt due to Sir William Parsons, for his colleague, Sir John Borlase, was too old and too indolent to exercise much influence. Parsons, as his later conduct shows, disliked and distrusted Ormond; but on this occasion his rejection of Ormond's advice was probably due to caution rather than to ill-will, for so far none of the English reinforcements, promised as soon as news of the insurrection reached London, had arrived. This delay was due to the political situation in England. The dispute between king and parliament had now reached a stage at which a peaceful settlement seemed almost impossible; and the house of commons was unwilling to trust the king with the means of raising an army that might, they feared, eventually be used against themselves. It was not until the very end of 1641 that some English troops reached Dublin; and though more followed during the next few months, the total fell far short of what was needed, for by that time the insurrection had spread beyond Ulster and was soon to involve the whole country.

Ormond's proposal to attack the insurgents may have been rash; but the more cautious policy followed by Parsons proved disastrous. By the end of November the Ulster forces had moved south into Leinster, captured Dundalk and were preparing to besiege Drogheda, barely thirty miles north of Dublin. In these circumstances the Old English nobility and gentry of the area, finding that the lords justices were unable to protect them and unwilling to provide them with arms so that they might protect themselves, decided that their only safe course was to join the insurgents, with whose demand for religious toleration they were, naturally, in full agreement. But before doing so they secured from the Ulster leaders a formal and public declaration of their loyalty to the crown. It was not long before this example was followed by the Old English of Munster and Connaught; and in the course of 1642 there came into being a Catholic Confederacy, with its capital at Kilkenny, in which all four provinces were united.[1] In this way an insurrection that had begun among the native Irish of Ulster was transformed into a national movement led by the Old English aristocracy. They it was who dominated the Assembly, which was the parliament of the confederacy, and the Supreme Council, which was its executive.

For Ormond this defection of the Old English meant that most of his relations and many of his close friends were now ranged on the opposite side. This certainly did not weaken his determination to suppress rebellion and restore the authority of the crown; but it may well have strengthened his distaste for the kind of warfare on which Parsons and his supporters in the council insisted. They refused to allow him to undertake a regular campaign. Instead, they sent him on expeditions through the countryside with instructions

> to wound, kill, slay and destroy, by all the ways and means
> he may, all the said rebels, their adherents and relievers,
> and burn, spoil, waste, consume, destroy and demolish all
> the places, towns, and houses where the said rebels are, or
> have been relieved and harboured, and all the corn and hay
> there, and kill and destroy all the men there inhabiting able
> to bear arms.

Ormond, who had no taste for this sort of work, interpreted his instructions as narrowly as possible and was criticized for his moderation. Some of his subordinates, however, had no such scruples

1. This confederacy has been commonly called the Confederation of Kilkenny; but this term was not used by contemporaries.

and were praised and encouraged. When Sir Charles Coote - a brave and successful soldier, but noted for his brutality, even in that brutal age - hanged without trial a prisoner who was under Ormond's special protection, the council refused, despite Ormond's insistent demands, to allow any action to be taken against him.

Though Ormond did what he could to moderate the harsh measures prescribed by the council and to restrain the brutality shown by some of his subordinates, it was not unnatural that the insurgents should hold him responsible, as lieutenant-general of the army, for all that was done. In February 1642, after one of his expeditions through Leinster, he received a message from Lord Gormanston, a leader among the Old English insurgents, accusing him of cruelty and warning him that 'the best pledges he had, which was his wife and children, should answer for it, if he did make any more such journeys'. Ormond was very anxious to reply both to the accusation and to the threat; but he knew that if he did so on his own responsibility his enemies in Dublin would seize upon his action as evidence that he was in communication with the rebels. To avoid this danger he brought the matter before the council; and it was with the council's consent that he returned his answer. In this, he first rebuts the charge of cruelty, though making it clear that rebels have no right to complain and that he himself is under no obligation to justify his conduct to Gormanston. As for the threat, he admits that his wife and children are in the power 'of some who have been cozened out of their loyalty'; but, he continues, 'if they shall receive injury by men, I shall never revenge it upon women and children; which, as it would be base and unchristian, would be extremely below the price I value my wife and children at'.

Gormanston's threat may not have been seriously meant; but it must have seemed serious enough to Ormond, for at this time his wife and children were still at Carrick, which was now in the hands of insurgents. In fact, however, they seem to have been quite safe; and Lady Ormond was not only allowed to live peacefully in her own house but also to shelter scores of distressed protestants who, less fortunate than herself, had been driven from their homes and despoiled of their goods. A few weeks after Ormond's firm reply to Gormanston she was permitted to remove to Dublin, accompanied by her children and by a great crowd of refugees whom she had protected; and in Dublin the number of those who depended on her bounty was greatly increased.

25

When Lady Ormond reached Dublin, early in April, Ormond was not there to welcome her. He had been sent on an expedition through County Kildare with a force of 3,000 foot and 500 horse. Though his orders were, as usual, to destroy the property of rebels, the main purpose on this occasion was to reinforce a number of outlying posts still held by government troops. This he accomplished successfully; but on the return march, his army now considerably reduced, he found his way blocked by an insurgent force twice as numerous as his own. Ormond had none of the rashness that one might expect in a young and inexperienced commander; and he would gladly have avoided battle if he could. But the nature of the terrain left him no choice. The way to Dublin lay through a narrow pass, at Kilrush, in County Kildare. It was to secure this pass that Ormond was obliged to fight; and here, on 15 April 1642, he had his first experience of a pitched battle. As a battle it did not, indeed, amount to very much. The insurgents, though strong in numbers, were badly led, ill-disciplined and divided by faction. Almost at the first onslaught they broke and fled, leaving behind them all their baggage, stores and colours. But Ormond's victory, though in fact it did no more than allow him to return safely to Dublin, greatly enhanced his prestige, in England as well as in Ireland. The English house of commons not only expressed its thanks in a letter from the speaker, Lenthall, but also voted the sum of £500 for a jewel to be presented to Ormond as a memorial of the occasion.

In his letter of thanks, written on 5 May, Ormond asked that further help should be sent to the army in Ireland

> that so our present and pressing wants of almost all things
> necessary for a war, prove not hindrances to our earnest
> desire of going on, through all oppositions and dangers, to
> the reducing of this kingdom to the obedience due to his
> Sacred Majesty and his laws.

When this letter was written the quarrel between king and parliament had already reached a stage at which civil war seemed likely; and had Ormond been in England he would have done all he could to support the royal cause. But as commander of the army in Ireland he knew that it was to parliament he must look for the supplies so urgently needed. Even after the outbreak of war in England, in August 1642, he joined with the lords justices and the council, of which he himself was a member, in maintaining a correspondence with Lenthall as well as the king. At the same time, however, he made no secret of his sympathy with the royalist cause; and this gave Parsons, who favoured the parliament, an additional reason for thwarting him. When the absentee lord lieutenant, the Earl of Leicester, sent over his son, Lord Lisle, a young man in his early twenties, as lieutenant-general of horse, Parsons did all he could to promote his interests, in the hope of seeing him replace Ormond as commander of the army.

It seemed at one time as if Parsons might have his way. In the late summer of 1642, which proved a very sickly season, Ormond fell ill of a fever and at one stage seemed unlikely to survive. Later on, after his recovery, he remarked wryly in a letter to a friend:

> Before I fell sick, all my propositions of going or sending forth upon service were answered by the emptiness of the store and the wants of the army; but when I was fast, then provisions were made for a three weeks expedition.

And Parsons made sure that the command of the expedition was given to Lisle.

While Ormond's life was actually in danger, however, he was much less concerned about the treatment he had received from Parsons than about the fate of his family if he should die. It was long since he had received any income from his estates, all of which were in the hand of the insurgents; and the payments due to him as lieutenant-general were heavily in arrear. He had pledged his credit to the utmost, not only to meet his household expenses - much enlarged by Lady Ormond's generous provision for refugees - but also, on occasion, to provide essential supplies for his troops. His death at this point would leave his wife and children destitute. In these circumstances he appealed to the king to take care of his family if he should die; and the king readily promised to do all he asked.

Charles was not called upon to perform this promise; but he found other ways of showing his appreciation of Ormond's services. In mid-September, when Ormond was well on the way to recovery, he received a new commission as lieutenant-general of the army, by which he was to hold his command directly from the king himself and not, as before, under the lord lieutenant. And in the same month he was made a marquess. These marks of royal favour certainly raised his prestige and increased his liberty of action. But so long as the lords justices controlled the money and the stores needed to mount a campaign he could do little without their co-operation; and Parsons remained as jealously suspicious of him as before.

The parliamentary authorities in England, perhaps encouraged by

Parsons' attitude, now sought to strengthen their influence in Dublin. Two commissioners appointed by them - Robert Goodwin and Robert Reynolds - arrived there in October 1642; and Parsons not only admitted them to meetings of the council but allowed them to take part in its deliberations. At the same time he encouraged a fanatical puritan preacher, Stephen Jerome, to make thinly-veiled attacks upon the royal family and upon Ormond in his sermons, a medium of political propaganda in common use at the time.

Ormond felt that he could afford to ignore the sermons; but he was alarmed at the attempts of Goodwin and Reynolds to win the support of the army for the parliamentary cause. They had brought with them £20,000; and, with ready cash to back up their arguments, they found some who were ready to listen to them. But, in the end, Ormond's influence prevailed. Those who had been at first inclined to follow the commissioners' lead now drew back; and a letter to the king, assuring him of their readiness to obey his commands, was signed by the army officers in Dublin and in all the other cities and garrisons under Ormond's control. The parliamentary commissioners were obliged to accept failure; and in February 1643 they left Dublin and returned to London.

(3)

While the parliamentary commissioners were still in Dublin the king had taken the first step towards making peace, or at least a truce, with the Confederate Catholics; and it is likely that he already had in mind the possibility of bringing over a considerable part of the army then under Ormond's command to support the royalist cause in England. On 11 January 1643 he signed a commission to Ormond and six others, instructing them to meet with representatives of the Confederate Catholics, receive a written statement of their grievances and forward it to him for his consideration. But in the meantime there was to be no cessation of hostilities, save for the issue of a safe conduct to the Confederate representatives. After a good deal of delay the proposed meeting took place at Trim, on 17 March; and this did in fact lead, though only after considerable delay, to the conclusion first of a truce and then of a peace treaty.

Ormond himself did not attend the meeting at Trim, though his tactful handling of the Confederates had done much to bring it about.

28

When it took place he was with the army in Wexford, on a campaign that had been undertaken as much to get the troops out of Dublin, where provisions were scarcer than ever, as to capture New Ross, which was its ostensible object. Ormond found New Ross too strong to be taken with the forces he had; his supplies were running short; and on 18 March he set off on the return march to Dublin. Within a few miles, at a point where the road passed through a narrow glen, he found his way blocked by a much larger army, under Thomas Preston, the Confederate commander in Leinster. Here, as at Kilrush, he had no choice but to fight. After a brisk engagement, in which Ormond's artillery proved very effective, the Confederates retreated in disorder, and did not rest until they had put the River Barrow between themselves and the enemy. No one has ever claimed that Ormond was a great soldier; and five years later he was to lose, with disastrous consequences to the royal cause in Ireland, the only decisive battle in which he was ever engaged. But on this occasion, though heavily outnumbered, he put to flight a veteran commander, who had won high distinction in the Spanish service and was already an experienced soldier before Ormond was born. All Ormond's victory brought him, however, was an open road to Dublin, where his return only increased the problem of finding food for the troops.

A little more than a month after Ormond's return to Dublin the king imposed upon him a new and heavy responsibility. By a commission dated 23 April 1643, addressed to Ormond alone, he was to treat with the Confederates 'with all secrecy and convenient expedition' for a cessation of hostilities for one year. The settlement of terms was left to his sole judgement, the king promising in advance to ratify whatever he might agree to. The purpose behind this commission is made clear by a message in cypher that accompanied it: once a cessation had been arranged Ormond was to bring over the army under his command to Chester.

Ormond knew that the parliamentary party in England and its supporters in Ireland would regard any truce with the Confederates as a betrayal of the protestant cause; and if they were to get the upper hand the king's commissions would hardly protect him against their resentment - he had, after all, the example of Strafford before him. He did what he could, however, to secure his position in advance. In June, while his negotiations with the Confederates were still at an early stage, he twice brought the matter before the council. He proposed, first, that if the council disapproved of a cessation it should express its opposition formally in letters to the king and should also propose 'some more certain, honourable and available way for the preservation of the kingdom, the safety of the protestant subjects and the subsistence of the armies'. In that event he would, on his own responsibility, break off his negotiations with the Confederates. Next day he made another offer: he would break off negotiations if the council could provide, within a fortnight, £10,000 for the support of the army. But the council was unwilling to oppose the king openly and unable to raise the money; and Ormond, having ensured that his offers were recorded, as a safeguard in case of any future criticism of his conduct, resumed the task of making a truce.

He was equally cautious in his dealings with the Confederates, scrupulously avoiding any terminology that might seem to imply that they were anything other than rebellious subjects seeking to be restored to the favour of their sovereign. Though the idea of a cessation had originated with the king, Ormond insisted that the first formal move should be made by the Confederates. It was, he felt, beneath the dignity of a king to make any approach to rebels; it was their place to approach him, in suitably humble terms, and ask him to grant them a truce. And throughout all his negotiations, first for a truce and later on for a treaty, he maintained the same attitude, which might well seem out of keeping with his relatively weak military position. His ability to do so owed something to the traditional respect that the Old English nobility and gentry, who dominated the Confederacy, had for the head of the Butler family. But it owed more to the Confederates' own sense of loyalty to the crown, a loyalty that was certainly not unconditional, but that was none the less genuine. At no point did they conceive of a final settlement that did not include their own restoration to the king's favour and the king's restoration to his lawful authority. This loyalty, based upon principle, was further reinforced by a conviction, which later events proved to be well-founded, that if the parliamentary cause triumphed in England their own position would become infinitely worse than it had been.

In his negotiations for a truce Ormond made full use of his advantages - his personal and family influence, the Confederates' desire to demonstrate their loyalty to the king and their fear of a parliamentary victory. He insisted throughout that the cessation was to be no more than a truce, during which the Confederates could put their case before the king and the two sides could endeavour to reach a comprehensive settlement. He refused, despite strong pressure from the Confederates, to include in the terms now to be arranged anything beyond what was necessary to establish and maintain a cessation of hostilities. In the end, he had his way; but the negotiations dragged on over several months; and it was not until 15 September 1643 that the cessation was at last signed. The terms were simple: each side was to retain the territory it held at the time of signing; there was to be an exchange of prisoners; safe conducts were to be granted to Confederate delegates so that they could travel to England and lay their grievances and proposals before the king. In the meantime, the Confederates were to pay the king, in compensation for his loss of revenue in the territory they held, £30,000, half in money and half in cattle.

To have secured a truce on these terms, without making any concession in return, was a very considerable achievement; and in November the king showed his appreciation of Ormond's services by appointing him lord lieutenant in place of the absentee Leicester. It was a post that Ormond certainly had not sought: the king had offered it to him almost a year earlier; and at that time he had begged to be excused. He accepted it now only from a sense of duty: the rewards of office were, in the circumstances, negligible; the difficulties and dangers were obvious and pressing; when he declared that nothing save the ambition of serving the king could induce him to accept it, he was using words that might have been merely formal; but they expressed what he really felt.

(4)

Several weeks elapsed before formal ratification of Ormond's appointment as lord lieutenant reached Dublin; and it was not until 21 January 1644 that he was sworn in, after the traditional fashion, in Christ Church Cathedral. The sermon was preached by the bishop of Limerick, Robert Sibthorp, who took as his text the last verse of the seventy-seventh psalm: *Thou leddest thy people like a flock by the hand of Moses and Aaron.* On this text, we are told by a contemporary, 'he paraphras'd exceeding elegantly'; but there was little probability that the people whom the king had entrusted to Ormond's guidance would obediently follow their shepherd.

One effect of the cessation had been to create division among Irish protestants. Up to this time, with whichever side they might sympathize in the English civil war, they had stood together against the common enemy at home; and this unity might still have survived but for the action of the English parliament and their Scottish allies, who immediately condemned the cessation and urged protestants to continue the war. For some months the issue was doubtful; but by March 1644 the protestant forces in Ulster had resolved, despite all Ormond's efforts to dissuade them, to resume hostilities. A few months later, in July, the protestant commander in Munster, Lord Inchiquin, followed this example, acting now under the authority of the English parliament.

Despite this renewal of hostilities in two of the four provinces, the cessation remained in force so far as Ormond and the Confederates were concerned. The Confederates were genuinely anxious for a treaty that would remove their grievances and restore them to the position of loyal subjects of the crown. After the cessation they had sent agents to Oxford, where the king then was; but the discussions there had led to no result and the task of concluding a definitive treaty of peace had been left to Ormond. Negotiations dragged on for months without any real progress being made, for Ormond found it impossible to get clear instructions from the king. Time after time he asked for guidance as to what concessions he might make; but his requests were either ignored or answered only in general terms. George Digby, the king's secretary of state, recognized that Ormond was in a difficult position; but he held out no hope of his receiving the detailed instructions for which he asked. The substance of what he had to say in response to Ormond's appeal is expressed in a single sentence:

> The case therefore in short is this: the king hath committed
> that kingdom to your care, prudence and fidelity, and you
> are to manage it according to your best discretion, with the
> help of the best lights we can possibly give from hence, but
> with very little of commands or directions.

It was almost certainly his disappointment at not receiving the guidance he had asked for that led Ormond, in November 1644, to beg the king to relieve him of the viceroyalty. But the king refused to do so. He thanked Ormond warmly for his services to the crown and assured him that they would be amply rewarded; but, in the meantime, he was to remain in office and do all he could do to conclude a lasting peace.

During the next three months Ormond and the Confederates continued to exchange views, without making much progress towards a definitive settlement. But in February 1645 there was a radical change in the position. By that time the king's fortunes had so far declined that he became eager for help, from whatever source it might come; and the source that seemed to him most hopeful was Ireland. The Confederates might, he thought, be willing, in return for substantial concessions on his part, to send an army to support his cause in England. In February 1645 he wrote to Ormond, commanding him to make peace with the Confederates on almost any terms, 'so that freely and vigorously they engage themselves in my assistance against my rebels of England and Scotland'. He placed two restrictions only on the terms to be made: the security of his protestant subjects in Ireland must not be endangered and his own regal authority must be preserved.

It might seem that on this basis Ormond should have been able to conclude a treaty with little delay. But there were still difficulties to be overcome. In the first place, the king had told him to make the best bargain he could and not, save in the last resort, to reveal the terms of these new instructions. In the second place, clerical influence had become so strong among the Confederates that they could no longer be satisfied by the suspension or repeal of the penal laws; and the demands that they now put forward with respect to church property and the status of their clergy were such that Ormond felt bound to reject them. As a result, there did not seem to be much prospect of a speedy settlement. But in the meantime, and without Ormond's knowledge, the king had entrusted the task of securing military help from the Confederates to another agent, the Earl of Glamorgan, who arrived in Dublin early in August 1645.

Though Glamorgan's mission was a secret, he came openly to Dublin, ostensibly on his own private affairs, and bringing a letter to Ormond from the king, recommending him as a person who might possibly be useful in negotiations with the Confederates. On the surface, all seemed natural enough. Glamorgan's Irish connections - his second wife, Margaret O'Brien, was a daughter of the Earl of Thomond - would account for his visit to Dublin; and the fact that he was himself a Roman Catholic would make him acceptable to the Confederates. Ormond certainly did not suspect that he had any purpose beyond what he openly stated; and his suspicions, had he had any, would have been done away by a postscript, in cypher, that the king had added to his letter: 'His honesty or affection to my service will not disappoint you; but I will not answer for his judgement'. Ormond could hardly suppose that the king would put secret negotiations into the hands of a man whose judgement he could not trust.

On the strength of the king's recommendation Ormond had no hesitation in allowing Glamorgan to take part in discussions with the Confederate agents then in Dublin or, later, in allowing him to accompany them on their return to Kilkenny. Once there Glamorgan quickly let the Confederates know that he had the king's authority to conclude peace with them. Since he had none of Ormond's scruples about making concessions in matters of religion, agreement was soon reached; and on 25 August a treaty was signed. Glamorgan guaranteed, on the king's behalf, that the Roman Catholics should enjoy free and public exercise of their religion, that they should retain all churches and church property possessed by them since 23 October 1641, and that they should have possession of all other churches not actually in protestant hands at the time the treaty was made. In return, the Confederates promised to equip 10,000 men for the king's service; and the treaty was to remain secret until this force had landed in England. During the interval negotiations with Ormond were to continue as before.

His task completed, Glamorgan returned to Dublin. While at Kilkenny he had maintained a correspondence with Ormond and had written optimistically about the prospects for a satisfactory settlement; but he had not, of course, given the slightest hint of the business in which he was engaged. When Ormond renewed negotiations with the Confederates, in September, he did so in total ignorance of the fact that they already felt themselves secure of better terms than any he was likely to concede. To the Confederates, indeed, the resumption of negotiations at this stage was important mainly as a means of ensuring that Ormond should not become suspicious of their dealings with Glamorgan. But it is likely that some of them foresaw the possibility that the king might find himself obliged to disown the Glamorgan treaty, and that a settlement with Ormond, though on less favourable terms, might prove more secure. Very soon, however, the whole situation was transformed by the arrival on the scene of a new actor. On 12 November a papal nuncio, Giovani Baptista Rinuccini, landed in Kerry; and a month later he was at Kilkenny.

Rinuccini was a single-minded ecclesiastic, imbued with the spirit of the Counter-reformation and determined to assert his authority as the pope's representative. Between him and Ormond no compromise was possible; and the Confederates were obliged, in the long run, to side with one or the other. To begin with, it seemed as if Rinuccini was to have his way. Glamorgan, who visited him shortly after his arrival at Kilkenny, assured him that the king was prepared to make further concessions; and together they agreed on important additions to the treaty that Glamorgan had already made with the Confederates.

This new treaty was concluded on 20 December 1645; and on Christmas Eve Glamorgan arrived back in Dublin. But during his absence a copy of the treaty he had made in August had come into Ormond's hands;[1] and on 26 December he was brought before the council. He defended what he had done; but was careful not to say anything that might involve the king; and Ormond, who probably suspected that the king was more deeply concerned than it would be safe to disclose, soon released him. The king himself, when news of the affair reached London, at once repudiated Glamorgan's negotiations with the Confederates, both publicly and in letters to Ormond and the council in Dublin. This was almost certainly unfair to Glamorgan; but it helped to convince the Confederate leaders that if they were to make peace they must do so through Ormond.

This seems to have been the view taken by Ormond himself. In an undated memorandum - which must, however, belong to the early months of 1646 and which was probably intended for the king - he argues that if the Confederates insist on the terms of the Glamorgan treaty then the king has nothing to gain from a peace from them. Should he, in consequence, 'give them up a sacrifice to his own safety, the sin of their extirpation will be equally shared betwixt the parliament, that covet their land and thirst for their blood, and themselves, that will accept of no conditions but such as for no earthly consideration his Majesty can grant, or any honest protestant minister of his be an instrument to convey to them...'. Ormond may have secretly feared that Charles, in an extremity, would yield what the Confederates demanded on behalf of their church; but there can be no doubt that he himself was resolved to play the part of an 'honest

1. The copy had been found on the body of Archbishop O'Queely of Tuam, who had been killed in a skirmish near Sligo in October 1645.

protestant minister'.

For the time being, however, the Supreme Council of the Confederates, impressed by the firmness with which the king had disowned Glamorgan's negotiations, were prepared to modify their demands; and Ormond was able to conclude a treaty of peace without having to concede any more than he had already offered. There was to be a general pardon for all offences since the outbreak of the insurrection in 1641; an oath of allegiance was to take the place of the oath of supremacy, which meant that recusants would now be eligible for posts under the crown; estates confiscated during Strafford's regime were to be restored. These were the most important terms of the treaty signed on 28 March 1646; but a clause by which the consideration of further concessions in matters of religion was left to the king held out a hope that more might be conceded. The Confederates, for their part, undertook to provide 10,000 troops for the king's service in England. But when the treaty was signed Chester, the last port in the king's hands, had fallen to the parliamentary forces and the Confederate troops remained in Ireland.

At the time of the signing of the treaty the Supreme Council had agreed that it should be published at a date to be settled by Ormond, but not earlier than 1 May. They knew that Rinuccini and his supporters would condemn the ecclesiastical provisions as inadequate; and they hoped that during the interval the king might be induced to make further concessions. Ormond himself was in no hurry, for he too was uneasy about Rinuccini's attitude; but in June the Supreme Council, having given up hope of better terms, asked Ormond to have the peace proclaimed without further delay. He was quite willing to do so; but on 24 June, before the necessary arrangement had been completed, he received a letter from the king that upset all his plans. In this letter the king ordered him 'to proceed no further in treaty with the rebels, nor engage us upon conditions with them after sight hereof'. This reduced Ormond almost to despair. He knew that the king was now in the hands of the Scots; and he might reasonably suppose that the letter did not represent his real wishes; but he could hardly act directly contrary to such an explicit command. After consultation with the council he wrote to the king, on 29 June, setting out the consequences that would follow if he acted according to these instructions. The cessation of arms agreed upon in September 1643 had been renewed from time to time; but unless he were allowed to treat with the Confederates for a further extension it would terminate on 13 July and the war would be renewed. The Confederates had three armies in the field, one of them within a few days' march of Dublin; and he could not hope to defend the city successfully unless he speedily received 'a competent supply of men, money, victuals, clothes, shoes, arms, ammunition'.

Ormond did not exaggerate the desperate weakness of his military position; but he must have known that the king had no means of supplying the reinforcements and supplies for which he asked so urgently. It is not unfair to assume that his purpose was, in the first place, to put pressure on the king to sanction further negotiations with the Confederates and, in the second, to provide in advance justification of his own conduct should he be obliged, by a renewal of hostilities, to abandon Dublin. But a few days later the difficulty created by the king's new instructions was removed by Digby, who arrived in Dublin on 4 July. He assured Ormond that the king had managed, despite the vigilance of the Scots, to send a message to the queen, warning his supporters not to accept as genuine any order from him unless it were in cypher in his own hand, or else conveyed through the queen or the prince of Wales. Ormond might, therefore, safely disregard the letter he had received and complete his arrangement for the publication of the treaty. Despite Digby's assurance, some members of the council were reluctant to go against the king's written instructions on the strength of a verbal message; but Ormond, in characteristic fashion, got round the difficulty by taking the whole responsibility upon himself and having a statement to this effect entered in the council records. With this last difficulty out of the way, peace was formally proclaimed in Dublin on 30 July; and on 3 August the Supreme Council proclaimed it in Kilkenny.

The publication of the peace marked Ormond's completion of a task entrusted to him by the king more than two years earlier. But during that interval the situation had changed radically. It was too late now for this treaty with the Confederates to be of any service to the king's cause in England; and it was doubtful if it would even bring peace in Ireland. Rinuccini was certain to condemn it; and his influence might well prove stronger than that of the Supreme Council. Ormond had foreseen this danger and had done what he could to win support for the treaty from the two Confederate generals whose opposition he most feared. Thomas Preston, commander of the Leinster Army, had readily agreed to abide by the terms of peace and to act under Ormond's orders. But Owen Roe O'Neill, who commanded the Ulster army, was fully committed to Rinuccini; and though he professed his loyalty to the king, as he constantly did until his death four years later, he took his orders from the nuncio. It was O'Neill's attitude that settled the fate of the treaty. At this time his prestige stood very high, for in June, at Benburb in County Tyrone, he had inflicted a crushing defeat on the Scottish army in Ulster. Then, at Rinuccini's bidding, he had led his victorious army southwards to overawe the Supreme Council. Preston, whether inspired by this example or frightened by a threat of excommunication, soon afterwards broke his engagement with Ormond and placed himself and his army under the nuncio's orders.

Despite Rinuccini's uncompromising attitude and the clear evidence that he had widespread and powerful support, the Supreme Council still hoped that the peace could be saved; and it was in the belief that Ormond's personal influence would prove decisive that they urged him to come to Kilkenny. In the letter of invitation that they sent him Richard Bellings, secretary to the council and an old friend of Ormond, assured him that 'nothing will settle warring dispositions so much as your lordship's presence here'. Ormond, willing to try any means of strengthening support for the treaty, accepted the invitation; and on 31 August he entered the city that had long been the principal seat of his family but that he had not seen for almost five years. As a mark of his confidence in the Supreme Council and the citizens he left the small force that he had brought with him from Dublin at Gowran, five miles off, and he entered the city with a bodyguard of eight men. The corporation, determined to show their loyalty to the king's representative and their devotion to the Butler family, had decorated the streets; and Ormond rode under arches displaying the achievements of his ancestors. But even in Kilkenny the authority of Rinuccini was evident. He had decreed that every city and town that accepted the peace should be placed under an interdict; and all the churches were, as Ormond noted, shut up.

Ormond soon became convinced that the Supreme Council could do little or nothing towards securing general acceptance of the peace throughout the country; and he decided that he must make a direct approach to Rinuccini. With this object he left Kilkenny and went to Carrick, within easy reach of Waterford, where Rinuccini then was. It proved a waste of time: Rinuccini ignored his proposal for negotiation; and after waiting some days for an answer that did not come he set out on the return journey to Kilkenny. But in his eagerness to secure a lasting peace he had placed himself in a dangerous position. Before he had travelled far he was warned that O'Neill and his army were approaching, with the object of cutting him off from Dublin; and since he had only a small force with him he had no choice but to make what haste he could in order to avoid capture. Nevertheless, when he came within a few miles of Kilkenny he paused and sent a message to the mayor and aldermen, offering to help them in defending the city against O'Neill. But they had no thought of resisting the Ulster army; and they advised him to continue his journey to Dublin. This he did without further delay, for O'Neill's much larger force was now dangerously near; and it was only by a hasty retreat that he was able to reach Dublin, on 13 September, without being forced to fight.

Though Ormond had arrived almost as a fugitive, his entry into the city was marked by the usual ceremonial; and, as an indication of the Supreme Council's submission to his authority, the sword of state was carried before him by Lord Castlehaven, one of the few Confederate commanders who dared to defy Rinuccini. This observance of customary forms, even at a time of crisis, reflected Ormond's determination to maintain an outward show of confidence; but he knew very well how nearly desperate the position was. Military stores were almost exhausted; there was no reserve of food, and if the city were cut off from the surrounding countryside both garrison and citizens would soon face starvation. But he had no thought of surrender and set to work at once to make such preparation as he could for defence. The conduct of his enemies gave him an unexpected respite. Rinuccini seems to have thought that he could take Dublin whenever it suited him; and he postponed his attack until he had crushed his enemies in the Confederacy. With the support of O'Neill's army he had no difficulty in overawing Kilkenny. He dismissed the Supreme Council, imprisoned most of its members and appointed a new council with himself as president. Preston, despite his earlier acceptance of the peace, now submitted to clerical dictation: and his army as well as O'Neill's was at Rinuccini's disposal. These changes had taken time; and it was the end of September before Rinuccini was ready to begin his advance on Dublin.

Ormond had used the interval to strengthen the fortifications of the city by building earthworks - a task in which women, including Lady Ormond, assisted the men. But he was convinced that the best, if not the only, hope of making a successful defence lay in securing reinforcements of men and supplies, wherever they might be had. 'The laws of nature and self-preservation', he wrote in a letter to Lord Clanricard, 'directed us to seek the readiest help we could think of'. His first application was to the Scottish forces in Ulster, for he knew that they were better disposed towards the king now that he was helpless than they had ever been while he could defend himself. But though they were willing to send troops to Drogheda, which was in no immediate danger, they would do nothing for Dublin. He also sent agents to London with an offer, on specified conditions, to transfer Dublin to the English parliament. The conditions he laid down reflect his guiding principles during this period. They were designed to secure the rights of the established church and to protect the Roman Catholic population, except for those who had been involved in the insurrection of 1641 and those who had rejected the peace of 1646; and the transfer was not to take place until it had been sanctioned by the king. But before any help from England could be expected the Confederate forces had advanced within striking distance of Dublin and had established their headquarters at Lucan, only a few miles from the city. From here they sent their demands to Ormond, threatening - at least by implication - that unless these were met they would attack immediately. But it was very doubtful if they were in a position to do so. Their arrangement for maintaining food-supplies had broken down; the health of the troops had suffered from a long spell of wet and stormy weather; and, besides this, O'Neill and Preston were now on such bad terms that Rinuccini had difficulty in preventing an open breach between them.

This was the state of affairs when, on 16 November, the two generals met in council with Rinuccini to debate what measures should be taken to improve their condition. While they sat together came the startling news that a parliamentary force had arrived in Dublin. With hardly a moment's delay O'Neill abandoned the consultation, assembled his forces and retreated. Rinuccini speedily followed his example; and, at least for the time being, Dublin was safe.

The report that had frightened the Confederate generals into a hasty withdrawal was not strictly accurate. Parliamentary ships had indeed, arrived at Dublin; but neither men nor supplies had been landed. The commissioners in charge of the expedition had come ashore and had been received by Ormond. But when he found that they had no authority to accept the conditions he had laid down and that the king had not even been consulted, he refused to transfer the city to their custody; and after some days spent in fruitless discussion they carried their troops and stores to strengthen the parliamentary forces in Ulster.

The retreat of the Confederates had removed the immediate threat to Dublin; but the prospects for the future were gloomy. The surrounding countryside, on which the city normally depended for much of its food supply, had been eaten bare by the Confederate armies; trade was almost at a stand-still; Ormond had no money to pay his troops and great difficulty in feeding them. It seemed to be no more than a matter of time before his government must collapse from lack of means to support it, even if the enemy launched no new attack. Since he was determined not to accept the terms that the nuncio had sought to impose and since it was clearly his duty to do what he could for the troops under his command and for the civilian population of the areas that he controlled, he had no choice but to make a new approach to the English parliament. Like most people at the time, he believed that king and parliament were bound to come to terms sooner or later and when that happened Dublin would return to its natural allegiance. But he did not act hastily; for he still hoped that those of the Confederate leaders who had opposed Rinuccini might recover their influence; and it was not until February 1647, when it was clear that Rinuccini's authority could not be shaken, that he made a formal offer to surrender Dublin and the other garrisons under his command on the terms offered by the parliamentary commissioners three months earlier and that he had then rejected.

Parliament accepted the offer; but, mindful of the breakdown of the negotiations some months earlier, insisted that he should send hostages, including one of his own sons, as a guarantee that the transfer would be completed. The preliminary arrangements took up some weeks; and it was not until the end of March that the first contingent of parliamentary troops arrived; and it was not until 7 June that commissioners empowered to take over authority from Ormond reached Dublin. Next day he sent instructions to the commanders of the garrisons under his control that they should henceforth act under the authority of the commissioners and admit such troops as they might send. It was, perhaps, in order to maintain at least an outward show of royal authority that he dated these instructions from 'His Majesty's castle of Dublin'.

Negotiations between Ormond and the commissioners continued for more than a week; and on 19 June agreement was reached. Protestants and such Roman Catholics as had not joined with the Confederates were to be left in peaceful possession of their property. Noblemen, gentlemen and officers who wished to accompany Ormond when he left the country were to be free to do so. Ormond was to make a formal surrender of his authority to the commissioners not later than 28 July, and earlier, on four days' notice, if they desired it. He was to receive from the commissioners a sum sufficient to discharge the debts that he had incurred, on his personal security, for the support of the army. The wording of this financial clause was designed to protect Ormond from any suspicion of having surrendered Dublin in return for a bribe. Indeed, the fear of laying himself open to such a charge had at first made him reluctant to accept any payment at all. But he was now reduced to such straits that had he refused this offer he would have been without any means of supporting his family or even of meeting the cost of going to London to give the king an account of the situation in Ireland.

From the time that he opened negotiations with the parliamentary authorities in February 1647 Ormond had foreseen that if he succeeded in coming to terms with them he would have to make this journey. It was no doubt with this in mind that he sent an order, in March, to his London tailor, William Perkins, for two suits of clothes; and these were dispatched a month later: a black suit and a grey one, each with a cloak to match. In a letter written at the same time Perkins reminded Ormond, very humbly, that he had not yet been paid for clothes supplied in 1641, so that the total amount now due came to £226-16-6. Ormond had little money to spare, but he must have managed to pay this bill in whole or in part; for a year later, though other suits for Ormond himself, his sons and his servants, had been ordered in the interval, the total amount due to Perkins had been reduced to £220.

When Ormond's new suits reached Dublin he was still awaiting the arrival of the parliamentary commissioners; and even after he had concluded his agreement with them, on 19 June, he remained for more than a month longer in the hope of receiving the full amount of the payment due to him. The business went very slowly and was still far from complete when the day arrived on which he was to make the formal surrender of the viceroyalty and quit the Castle. The commissioners were now anxious for his departure; he himself was reluctant to remain after he had lost even the outward show of office; and on 28 July he took ship for England, leaving Lady Ormond to receive what was still due to him and to make the best bargain she could with those who had advanced money for the royal service on his security.

CHAPTER IV

Ireland: The Last Stand, 1647 - 1650

(1)

On 2 August 1647 Ormond landed at Bristol. It was from Bristol that he had set sail for home, fourteen years earlier, a wealthy young nobleman, newly come into his inheritance and with every prospect of a happy life before him. Now he was little better than a fugitive; and, with the royal cause apparently in ruins, the outlook both for himself and for his family seemed gloomy. Lady Ormond had borne him eight sons and two daughters: but five of the sons - three of whom had been christened James after their father - had died in infancy. Of those who survived the eldest, Thomas, was barely thirteen, Richard was eight and John four. Elizabeth, the elder of the daughters, was seven and Mary, born in 1646, was still a baby. It was fortunate for Ormond that his wife was a strong-minded woman and well able to look after her family, for from this time onwards until the restoration of the monarchy in 1660 he himself was to see little of them.

From Bristol, Ormond went first to his uncle, Sir Robert Poyntz, at Acton; but he was eager to make his report to the king as soon as possible, and within a few days he was on his way to London. Since June, Charles had been in the hands of the army; and it was by permission of Fairfax, the commander-in-chief, that Ormond waited upon him at Hampton Court, where he had recently taken up residence. Ormond's purpose was not only to inform the king about the state of affairs in Ireland but also to justify his own conduct; and he left with him a lengthy account of the circumstances that had obliged him to surrender Dublin to the parliamentary commissioners. On this occasion Charles's manner, often stiff even with his most confidential advisers, seems to have been more gracious than usual. He declared himself entirely satisfied with all that Ormond had done and he rejected, with

45

a well-turned compliment, Ormond's offer to surrender his commission as lord lieutenant. Ormond's commitment to the monarchy was already so firm that it could hardly be strengthened; but the element of personal devotion evident in his later references to King Charles I may well have its source in this interview.

During the next few months Ormond remained in or near London, where Lady Ormond and the children joined him in September. But he could not devote much time to his family, for he was deeply involved in various abortive schemes for the revival of the royalist cause, including secret discussions with the commissioners whom the Scots had sent to negotiate with the king. These came to nothing; but before the end of the year the possibility of reviving the royalist cause in Ireland was unexpectedly renewed: Inchiquin, dissatisfied with his treatment by the English parliament, was preparing to change sides once more. In December Ormond returned to Acton, barely ten miles from Bristol, so that he might receive news of Irish affairs; and in January he sent an officer, Colonel John Barry, to negotiate with Inchiquin. There was another respect also in which the Irish situation looked hopeful. Rinuccini's influence was declining; and it seemed not unlikely that the Confederates would now be willing to make peace without allowing him to dictate the terms. Ormond, if anyone, could take full advantage of this new situation; and in January 1648 he received authority from the king to negotiate a new peace, provided that it could be done 'without ruining conscience and honour'.

Ormond's only safe route to Ireland was by way of France. But he would, in any case, have had to go there first. He needed money to finance his expedition; and the only person from whom he could hope to get it was the queen, who was then in Paris. His departure was hastened by the action of the parliamentary authorities: on 15 February they required him to give a written undertaking that while he remained in England he would do nothing that should be of disservice to their cause. It was clear that if he were to avoid arrest he must go at once. He managed to make his way to Hastings without arousing any suspicion; from there he crossed to Dieppe; and early in March he joined the queen and the Prince of Wales in Paris.

(2)

Ormond was detained in France much longer than he had expected, for the business of raising funds to finance his return to Ireland went very slowly. The queen had realized a considerable sum by the sale of her jewels; but Lord Jermyn, who managed her financial affairs, was very unwilling that anyone other than himself should have the spending of it. The result was that Ormond was kept waiting month after month; and, in the end, he got very much less than he had hoped for. In one respect, however, his presence in Paris at this period proved, at least from his own point of view, very fortunate. By the end of 1647 the Confederates had been so heavily defeated by the parliamentary forces in Munster and Leinster that they were now anxious to come to terms with the king, even if it meant defying Rinuccini. In April 1648 envoys appointed by them arrived in Paris to present their case to the queen; and Ormond was able to ensure that the answers she returned to their proposals, though conciliatory in tone, made no concessions beyond those already included in the treaty of 1646. Had he not been present there were other advisers at hand who might have persuaded her to make promises that would have dangerously restricted his own freedom of action, when six months later, he undertook the task of negotiating a definitive peace.

It was not until early in August that he at last received a firm promise of payment; and then the sum offered - 3,600 pistoles, or about £3,000 - was much less than he had hoped for; but he thought it better to take it and go than delay any longer; for a warship, provided by the Prince of Orange, was now lying at Le Havre, ready to carry him and his party to Ireland. On 11 August he set off, leaving his brother-in-law, Sir George Hamilton, to collect the promised money and follow. Ormond had a good reason for making this early start. His wife and children had left England in June and were now living in Caen - chosen, probably, because it was one of the French cities in which the boys could receive a protestant education. He had visited them there already; but now he wished to bid them farewell before sailing for Ireland. By leaving Paris a few days ahead of Sir George Hamilton he could safely turn aside to Caen and yet be sure of reaching Le Havre in good time.

Ormond's visit to his family was a brief one; and he then made for the coast, intending to cross the estuary of the Seine to Le Havre by ferry the following morning. On the way, he fell in with the master of a small cargo-boat, who offered to take him over that evening; and this offer he gladly accepted. A change of wind delayed their progress and Ormond was growing impatient. When the master asked him what time it was he looked at his watch and then, hoping to encourage the man to make haste, told him it was an hour later than it actually was. This seems to be the only recorded occasion on which Ormond told a deliberate lie; and he soon paid for it. The master, misled about the time, not unnaturally misjudged the tide; the boat ran on a sandbank and split; and all on board narrowly escaped being drowned.

Ormond's haste to reach Le Havre proved to have been unnecessary as well as dangerous. When he arrived there Sir George Hamilton was still in Paris, awaiting the payment of the promised money; and it was not until many weeks later that he at last received it. The Dutch warship that carried Ormond and his friends to Ireland made a speedy passage when once it set sail; but, even so, it was not until 30 September that they landed at Cork. Very shortly after his arrival Ormond was in touch with Inchiquin, who was now fully committed to the royalist cause. But he was eager to open negotiations with the Confederates as soon as possible. Within a short time he went to his house at Carrick-on-Suir so as to be within easy reach of Kilkenny, where the Confederate assembly was then in session; and a few weeks later, at the request of the Confederates themselves, he moved to Kilkenny Castle. Though he was received with great enthusiasm on his arrival there, negotiations went very slowly. The Confederates were reluctant to accept less, in matters of religion, than had been promised them in the Glamorgan treaty; and this amounted to much more than Ormond was prepared to grant. He was restrained not only by his own conscientious scruples but also by the knowledge that the granting of such terms would alienate Inchiquin's strongly protestant troops. Some of them were, indeed, so much alarmed at any concessions to the Roman Catholic clergy that Ormond had been obliged to hurry back to Cork to allay their anxiety and prevent an open mutiny.

It seemed, at one time, as if the issue of religion would prevent any settlement at all. On 17 November, after weeks of discussion, Ormond wrote gloomily to Inchiquin about the most recent set of proposals put forward by the Confederates: 'I find some of them new... some of them impossible, and very many of them unreasonable'. In the end, it was events in England rather than negotiations in Kilkenny that brought the two sides together. Just three days after Ormond's letter to Inchiquin a 'Remonstrance of the army', drawn up by Ireton and approved by a council of officers, was presented to parliament, demanding that the king should be put on trial. It was not until 28 December that news of this threat to the king's life reached Kilkenny;

but when it came it brought a stronger sense of urgency into the negotiations. Ormond, though he still refused to give any guarantee about the future position of the Roman Catholic church, agreed that its clergy should retain the churches actually in their possession and should continue to exercise their jurisdiction until the matter had been considered in a free parliament. But he insisted, as he had always done, that the final decision must rest with the king. Beyond the introduction of the term 'jurisdiction' - to which he had previously objected - this made little advance on what he had offered before. But the Confederates, aware that the total overthrow of the monarchy would leave them face to face with a powerful and implacable enemy, were now willing to defy Rinuccini; and they accepted these terms as the best they could hope for in the circumstances.

With the question of religion out of the way, there was little difficulty in reaching a comprehensive settlement, by which the Confederates were restored to the position of loyal subjects of the crown. In these circumstances, they could have no reason for maintaining a distinct organization, with its own administrative system; and the terms of peace provided for the dissolution of the Confederacy, though the interests of those whom it represented were to be protected by the appointment of twelve 'commissioners of trust' who would assist Ormond in the government. The last formal act of the Confederate assembly, before its final dissolution, was to give unanimous approval to these articles of peace.

This was on 16 January 1649. Next day the members of the assembly, headed by their chairman, Sir Richard Blake, went to Kilkenny Castle, where they were received by Ormond, sitting on a throne of state. Blake laid the articles before him; and Ormond gave them his formal approval, as representative of the king. In the speech that he then made he called upon all present to fight for the cause of religion, 'not in the narrow circumscribed definition of it, by this, or that late found out term, but Christian religion'. He spoke of the danger in which the king stood, 'his life threatened to be taken away by the sacrilegious hands of the meanest of the people'. But he laid greatest weight on the need for unity among all who supported the king's cause, however much they might have been divided in the past:

> First, let me recommend to you, that in all holy causes (and such certainly is this) you will prepare yourselves with perfect charity that may obliterate whatever of rancour a

long-continued civil war may have contracted in you against
any that shall now co-operate with you in so blessed a
work.

In making this plea for unity among former enemies Ormond no
doubt had in mind not only Inchiquin, with whom the Confederates
had so recently been at war, but others also whom the threat to the
king's life might now bring over to the royalist side. More than six
weeks later, when he wrote to Secretary Nicholas reporting the
proclamation of Charles II in all cities and towns under his control,[1]
he was still hopeful that George Monck and Michael Jones, the
parliamentary commanders in Ulster and Leinster, might declare for
the king. But both rejected his advances; and the Scottish forces in
the north, though they stood by the monarchy, would make no alliances
with the Confederate Catholics. If all Ireland was to be brought under
the king's control it must be by war, not by negotiations.

(3)

For Ormond, the conclusion of peace with the Confederates was a
necessary preliminary to his main task, which was to re-establish the
king's authority throughout Ireland. For the Confederates, it was
essential that he should succeed if they were to derive any benefit
from the treaty they had made; and they had good reason to fear that a
parliamentary victory would reduce them to a worse position than
ever before. It was, then, in their own interest as well as in the
interest of the king that they should co-operate heartily with Ormond
in the campaign that he was preparing to open. But the unity of
purpose that had seemed dominant in January 1649 had merely
concealed for the time being the deep differences that divided them;
and these were later to emerge and make Ormond's task an impossible
one.

To begin with, however, what troubled him most was the difficulty
in finding money to maintain the troops that the Confederates,
according to the terms of the peace, had placed under his command.
The small sum that he had been able to raise in France had been
exhausted by the purchase of arms and by the cost of transporting
them, for which he had had to hire a ship; and when he landed at Cork
in September 1648 he had no more than thirty pistoles in his pocket.

1. Charles I had been executed on 30 January 1649.

The raising of money proved such a slow and difficult business that it was not until May that he was able to bring together his forces - amounting in all to 1,500 horse and 5,000 foot - and not until June that he was ready to open his campaign.

He established his camp at Finglas, a few miles north of Dublin; and here he was soon joined by Inchiquin with four thousand men. At first things went well: within a few weeks Inchiquin had driven the parliamentary garrisons from Drogheda, Dundalk, Newry and Trim. But Ormond's prime object was to take Dublin, not just because of its strategic importance but also because the re-establishment of the king's authority in the capital would strengthen the morale of the royalist party throughout the country. He did not feel strong enough to take the city by assault; and he realized that it would be very difficult - 'almost a desperate undertaking' was his own phrase - to reduce it by siege so long as the port remained open. In April he had appealed to Prince Rupert, who commanded a royalist fleet then based at Kinsale, to establish a naval blockade. But Rupert, who preferred the more profitable business of taking prizes, made no response; and he himself was soon afterwards penned up in Kinsale by a much stronger parliamentary fleet.

Despite this disappointment Ormond did not abandon hope. He moved the greater part of his army to Rathmines, south of Dublin, though he still left a substantial force on the north; and thus he cut off completely the city's communications with the surrounding countryside. This move certainly had some effect; and he was encouraged by reports of a growing scarcity of provisions in the city. But before the end of July the situation had changed to his disadvantage. Parliamentary ships arrived, bringing both supplies and reinforcements; the garrison of Dublin was now almost equal in numbers to the besieging army and distinctly superior in quality.

Almost at the same time as the garrison was strengthened the besiegers were obliged to divide their forces. It had been known for some time that the English parliament was preparing an army, under the command of Oliver Cromwell, to undertake the conquest of Ireland; and it had been generally assumed that this army would land at Dublin. Now came a rumour, probably designed to mislead the royalists, that the army would land in Munster. This put Ormond in a dilemma: even if he could take Dublin, which was at best doubtful, his success would be more than offset by a parliamentary conquest of Munster. In the end, he decided to send Inchiquin with a substantial force to guard the Munster coast, while he himself maintained the investment of Dublin.

Within a few days of Inchiquin's departure Ormond decided on a move that he might well have attempted earlier. Between his headquarters near Rathmines and the estuary of the River Liffey stood Baggotrath castle, which the parliamentary commander, Michael Jones, had not attempted to hold but had partially demolished. If the besiegers could occupy and re-fortify this post they would deprive Jones of the only grazing ground available for his cavalry and might also, by a further advance, command the approach to Dublin from the sea. Late at night, on 1 August, Ormond sent Major-General Patrick Purcell with 1,500 infantry and 800 pioneers to occupy the castle and repair the fortifications. He himself spent the night writing dispatches; and early the next morning he rode out to see how the work was progressing. To his surprise he found that it had scarcely begun: Purcell and his party had lost their way in the dark and had spent most of the night wandering about in search of the castle.[1] What was worse, Jones had become aware of Ormond's attempt to occupy this advanced post and had drawn out forces to prevent it.

Ormond must now decide, and decide quickly, whether to abandon his new position or defend it. He chose to defend it; and, in doing so, he knew that this must lead to a major engagement. 'I was confident', he wrote a few weeks later, 'that Jones would hazard all to interrupt our work, which [if it were] effected would so much annoy him'. It is clear from the orders he gave to the officers commanding horse and foot that he intended to remain on the defensive; and in the circumstances this was a reasonable decision. If he could retain and strengthen the new position he had occupied he would have gained a great and perhaps decisive advantage; and Jones, in attacking it, would have to advance up hill. But on two points his judgement was at fault: he underestimated the speed with which Jones would organize and launch his attack; and he assumed that the orders he had given would be fully and effectively obeyed without any further supervision on his part. 'With these orders I left them', he wrote some weeks later to his friend Lord Byron, 'determined to refresh myself with a

1. It is hard to understand how this happened. The castle was barely a mile from Ormond's headquarters; and Purcell himself had been there, with Ormond, the day before. There was a suspicion that the party had been deliberately misled; and some years later one of Ormond's numerous enemies among the Roman Catholic clergy was said to have claimed credit for having organized the trick.

little sleep for the action I expected, and in my way to my tent I caused all the regiments to stand to their arms'. He had, it is true, been up all night; but it is unlikely that either Inchiquin or Cromwell would have left the supervision of the final preparations for what he knew would be a decisive engagement to his subordinate officers.

It was nine o'clock in the morning of 2 August when Ormond retired to his tent. An hour later he was awakened by the sound of firing and rushed out to find his right wing, which stood nearest to Baggotrath Castle, broken and in flight. His attempt to make a stand in the centre failed; and the best he could do was to send off those regiments on his left wing that still held together to strengthen the garrisons of Trim and Drogheda, while he himself, with a disorderly following, made for Kilkenny, leaving his guns, his stores and his papers to the enemy. It was from Kilkenny that he sent the king, six days later, an account of the battle. He makes no attempt to disown responsibility for the defeat: 'I shall not go about to assign any reason for this misfortune, that may seem to lessen my share in it', he wrote; but he certainly did not regard it as disastrous and he expressed himself hopefully about the prospects for the royal cause in Ireland. It may, perhaps, have been to cheer Ormond up or, at least, to show that he had not lost favour at court, that Charles appointed him a Knight of the Garter in September, though the usual ceremony of installation had, in the circumstances, to be dispensed with.

(4)

The hopeful tone of Ormond's report to the king after the battle of Rathmines might seem, in retrospect, unrealistic. But at that time his position was still, in outward appearance, a strong one. His authority as lord lieutenant was recognized over the greater part of the country and the troops under his command were more numerous than the parliamentary forces, even after they had been strengthened by the arrival of Cromwell and his army in Dublin on 15 August. When, in October, Owen Roe O'Neill at last agreed to support the royalist cause Ormond might not unreasonably hope to recover all Ireland for the king. But before the end of the year the situation had changed. O'Neill died early in November; and his army, deprived of his leadership, played only a minor part in the war. Inchiquin's troops, never very happy about his alliance with Irish Catholics, had gone over to Cromwell; and though Inchiquin himself remained loyal to the king, Cork, Kinsale and Youghal, where his influence had once been dominant, readily accepted parliamentary garrisons. Despite these set-backs, Ormond strove for another twelve months to maintain the royalist cause in Ireland; and when, in December 1650, he gave up the struggle and left the country, it was not so much because of the military successes gained by the parliamentary forces, great though these were, as because the Catholic leaders, on whose support he must now depend, undermined his authority and made it impossible for him to continue the war.

The division among the Confederates created by Rinuccini had not been healed by the peace made in January 1649 and survived even after his departure from the country in the following month. The steady advance of Cromwell's army did nothing to promote unity: on more than one occasion the refusal of the rival parties to co-operate led to the loss of a post that might otherwise have been successfully defended. Early in December a meeting of bishops at Clonmacnoise issued an appeal for unity among all who supported the king, however much they might have differed in the past; but even the bishops themselves were not all of one mind, and their appeal had little effect. It was probably because of the failure of this attempt to bring the rival parties together that Ormond, a few weeks later, wrote to the king, describing the situation in which he was placed and asking for permission to leave Ireland should he find himself unable to exercise any effective authority. Royalist couriers must of necessity travel cautiously, often by circuitous routes; and it was not until the early spring of 1650 that Ormond received the king's reply, giving him the permission for which he asked. But he was reluctant to use it save as a last resort; and until almost the end of the year he endeavoured to maintain the struggle.

During the later months of 1649 the onset of winter had held up Cromwell's advance; but the weather was unusually mild for the time of year, and at the end of January he resumed operations. His steady advance disheartened many of the protestant gentry who still adhered to the king; they decided to leave Ireland and sent Michael Boyle, dean of Cloyne, to ask Cromwell for the necessary passes. These he readily granted; but he also induced Boyle to accept passes for Ormond and Inchiquin, though neither has asked for one. His purpose soon became clear: not long afterwards he tried to induce the governor of Waterford, which still held out against him, to capitulate, assuring him that Ormond himself was preparing to leave Ireland; and he sent, as evidence of this, a copy of the pass that he had induced Boyle to accept. By the time Ormond received the pass made out in his name he had already heard of the dishonest use that Cromwell had made of it. He sent the pass back; and the last sentence of the letter that accompanied it, though hardly likely to have any effect upon Cromwell, reflects Ormond's indignation at the trick that had been played upon him:

> I have by this trumpeter returned your paper, and for your
> unsought courtesy do assure you that when you shall desire
> a pass from me, and I think fit to grant it, I shall not make
> use of it to corrupt any that commands under you.

This letter was written on 17 May. A little more than a week later Cromwell was on his way back to England, leaving Ireton as commander in his place. Under him the campaign went more slowly; and to begin with he concentrated his attention on reducing the pockets of resistance that still remained in Ulster, Leinster and Munster.

Ormond was now confined to the territory west of the Shannon; and even here he had little effective authority. The bishops, most of whom had never been satisfied by the terms of the peace made in January 1649, now came out openly against him. In August they formally repudiated his authority; and a month later they issued a decree of excommunication against all who supported him. Almost at the same time Ormond's difficulties were further increased by the action of the king himself. Charles had been in Scotland since June; and in order to secure the help of a Scottish army he was prepared to accept any conditions that might be proposed to him. On 16 August, at Dunfermline, he signed a declaration that included, among other items, a formal repudiation of the peace made in his nåme with 'the bloody Irish rebels' and the recall of all commissions granted by him to any who had not signed the covenant. When news of this reached Ireland, Ormond insisted that the declaration must have been extorted from the king by unfair means and could therefore be ignored. But those who were already determined to get rid of him were not likely to be persuaded by such arguments; and Ormond soon decided that he had no option but to leave the country. The means of doing so were at hand, for a frigate, sent from Jersey by the Duke of York, was lying in Galway Bay; and on 6 December Ormond went on board, accompanied by Inchiquin and thirty or forty other officers.

Even those who had attacked Ormond most strongly were alarmed at the prospect of his imminent departure. The whole body of Confederates, clergy and laity alike, had always regarded the king, even when they were in rebellion against him, as the only legitimate source of secular authority - it was for this reason that they had been so anxious to come to terms with him. But if Ireland were now left without any duly appointed representative of the crown how was the framework of civil government to be held together? The idea of a sovereign authority derived from the people was alien to their thinking: even when, at an earlier stage, the bishops had demanded that Ormond should leave Ireland, they had demanded, at the same time, that he should make a formal transfer of his authority to men acceptable to them. But now, with Ormond actually on the point of departure, they were afraid that he would leave no one at all in his place. But Ormond, though only after some hesitation, felt obliged to make use of the authority given him by the king to appoint a deputy if he himself had to leave Ireland; and on 6 December he signed a commission appointing Ulick de Burgh, Marquess of Clanricard, to the office. Ormond had a high regard for Clanricard; and before making formal delivery of the commission he demanded and received from the bishops and leading laymen assurances that his authority as lord deputy would be respected; but he probably suspected, and Clanricard soon found, that these assurances were not to be depended upon. Then, after having done what he could to ease the task of his successor, Ormond set sail on 11 December. Three weeks later, after a tempestuous voyage, he and his companions landed in Brittany. On 9 January he reached Caen and was reunited with his family, none of whom he had seen for almost two and a half years.

CHAPTER V

Exile

(1)

The many years of exile that followed Ormond's arrival in France in January 1651 might seem, at first sight, to form a kind of hiatus in his long political career. For almost a decade he was engaged in one fruitless attempt after another to secure from France or Spain such military help as might enable the king to recover his crown; but the restoration of monarchy, when it came, was the product of internal developments in England and owed nothing to the efforts of Ormond and the other royalist exiles. And yet, though his unremitting labours on the king's behalf had been to all appearance fruitless, the years of exile marked a significant change in Ormond's position. Down to 1650 his service to the king, save for a brief period in 1647-8, had been confined to Ireland. He had never been at the centre of affairs and had had little or no share in the framing of policy. During the exile he became one of the king's principal advisers. Only Hyde, with whom he worked in close co-operation, had greater influence; and Hyde constantly consulted with Ormond on every matter of importance. Naturally, then, Ormond's position during the Restoration period was very different from what it had been in the 1640s. Now he could exert influence at the centre of power; and, though the weight of his influence varied considerably from time to time, he could seldom be altogether ignored so long as Charles II lived. Of all those who had held high office in the 1640s Ormond alone was still an influential figure forty years later.

After his arrival in France in January 1651 Ormond spent the greater part of a year with his wife and family at Caen; and his first concern was to provide for their future maintenance. He himself had only a few hundred pounds in hand and little prospect of more when that was exhausted. In July the Duke of York, who was lord high admiral, granted him a pension of 5,000 guilders a year out of the profits of Prince Rupert's semi-piratical fleet, which sold its prizes in

Dunkirk and the ports of northern France; but, though he later received some payments from this source, they were not to be counted upon and they fell far short of the amount promised by the duke. He might have recovered a part of his estate by coming to terms with Cromwell, as many other royalists did; but he was resolved to stand by the king to the end. He saw no reason, however, why he should not take advantage of the fact that about half the Ormond property belonged, by inheritance, to his wife; and she might come to terms with the parliamentary authorities without involving him. First, however, he asked the king's consent to what he proposed. This was readily granted; and Lady Ormond made her application. In September, Ormond could report to his brother-in-law, Lord Muskerry, that 'Cromwell hath given very civil answers... and there is nothing that keeps my wife from going to solicit this business but want of money to carry her thither, which I hope very shortly to get, and then she goes to keep life in her claim for herself and children... Upon this depends not our greatest but only visible hopes'.

Raising the funds necessary for the journey proved a long business; and almost a year passed before Lady Ormond went to London, taking her children with her. Here there was further delay. Cromwell was favourably disposed: no doubt he knew of her kindness to distressed protestants during the early stages of the insurrection. But, even so, it was not until February 1653 that instructions were issued to the commissioners responsible for the settlement of Irish estates, ordering them to let her have Dunmore House, a few miles north of Kilkenny, as a residence, and to assign her, out of the estates she had inherited from her parents, so much land as would provide an income of £2,000 a year. This, however, was by no means the end of the business; for the commissioners, whether through negligence or from ill-will, were very slow in providing sufficient land to yield the promised income. But Lady Ormond, with the welfare of her family at stake, refused to be satisfied with less than what was due to her; and at last she had her way. Ormond's wife and children were thus provided for; but great care had been taken to ensure that he himself should not receive any financial assistance as a result of the arrangement now made. The lands from which Lady Ormond's income was derived were put in the hand of trustees, who were instructed to 'take care that the profit of the premises, or any part thereof, be not disposed of to her husband'. Besides this, all correspondence between Lady Ormond and her husband was prohibited; and though this prohibition could sometimes be evaded it was sufficiently effective to be a sad deprivation to them both.

The knowledge that his family had a settled home and the means of maintaining it made it easier for Ormond to endure the poverty in which he himself must live; and he endured it without complaint. In Paris he habitually went about the city on foot, since he could seldom afford to ride in a coach. When he could not buy new clothes he made the best of the old. When he could not pay for his meals he was glad to get them on credit. He was not, of course, alone in his poverty. All the royalist exiles, with a very few exceptions, were in much the same condition: Sir Edward Hyde, King Charles's principal adviser, could not always afford a fire, even in the depth of winter. The king himself, though he was granted a pension by the French government and received occasional sums from other sources, was constantly in debt. Ormond had, indeed, one advantage over most of his fellow-exiles, for during the long years of warfare in Ireland he had become accustomed to hard fare and worn-out clothing.

(2)

It was in November 1651, while Lady Ormond's negotiations with Cromwell were still at an early stage, that Ormond joined the king in Paris. The two had met before, for at the time of Ormond's visit to Paris in 1648 Charles, then Prince of Wales, had been with his mother. But this second meeting marked the beginning of a new and much closer relationship. Charles, though not always wise in his choice of friends, was no bad judge of character; and he could recognize and appreciate Ormond's unselfish loyalty, his inflexible honesty and his sound common sense. When, a few months later, he appointed a council to consult together on his affairs Ormond was one of its five members; and it was Ormond's secretary, George Lane, who attended its meetings to keep a record of the decisions reached. In practice, however, the council was concerned mainly with formal business. On all matters of real importance the king sought guidance from two of its members: one was Ormond and the other Sir Edward Hyde, afterwards Earl of Clarendon. Throughout the whole period of the exile they remained his most intimate advisers; and they exercised more influence on his decisions than anyone else.

Though these two differed considerably in background and in character, they co-operated easily, bound together not only by common devotion to the king but also by mutual confidence and respect. Twenty years earlier they had known each other in London, before Ormond, then Lord Thurles, had come into his inheritance, and when Hyde was a young lawyer trying to make his way in the world. And so, wrote Hyde long afterwards, 'when they now met at Paris, they met as old friends, and quickly understood each other so well, that there could not be a more entire confidence between men'. Hyde may have exaggerated the extent of their earlier connection - 'a great acquaintance' he calls it - to which Ormond makes no reference. But after their meeting in Paris in 1651 they certainly worked together heartily in the king's service. Hyde was essentially a man of business; almost all the royal correspondence passed through his hands, and his regular place was at the king's headquarters, wherever that might happen to be. Ormond, active and resourceful, could safely be entrusted with an important mission, however delicate or dangerous; and on several occasions he was employed in this way.

One of the earliest of these missions was undertaken in November 1654, a few months after Charles, accompanied by his principal advisers, had transferred his residence from Paris to Cologne. At the urgent request of Henrietta Maria he had agreed that his younger brother - Henry, Duke of Gloucester - then a boy of fifteen, should remain with her in Paris. But, knowing her zeal in winning converts to Rome, he made her promise that she would do nothing to undermine the duke's protestant faith. Before long, however, the queen's zeal proved stronger than her honour. She urged upon the duke the advantages, temporal as well as spiritual, that he would gain by changing his faith; and, when he proved obstinate, she had him removed from Paris, separated from all his friends and placed under the care of an English Benedictine. When news of these doings reached the king he was both angry and alarmed. Though it is unlikely that he cared much about the theological issues involved, he knew that the conversion of his brother to popery would do incalculable damage to the royalist cause in England. He wrote at once both to the queen and the duke, upbraiding the one and encouraging the other. But the matter was much too serious to be settled by correspondence: someone must go to Paris and bring the duke away. The task called for a man high in rank and reputation, whom the queen could neither ignore nor browbeat, and, besides this, a man of cool judgement who could be trusted to manage the business with the least possible fuss and publicity. Ormond was the obvious choice; and he was soon on his way back to Paris.

His arrival there changed the situation. The king's commands, delivered by such a messenger, could not be disregarded: the duke was soon set at liberty and restored to the care of his protestant tutor. But Ormond, though he had won an initial success, soon found himself in an awkward situation. Hitherto the duke had been maintained at his mother's expense; now she disowned any further responsibility for him. He was turned out of the room he had hitherto occupied in her apartments in the Louvre and told that he must find bed and board elsewhere. This meant that Ormond, who was hard put to it to provide for himself, must now provide for the duke as well. From this difficulty he was rescued by Lord Hatton, who was somewhat better off than most of the royalist exiles in Paris. He spontaneously offered to provide accommodation for the duke, though he knew that he would incur the dangerous hostility of the queen by showing any kindness to her son.

This solved Ormond's most urgent problem; but another remained. He was to conduct the duke to Cologne; and he must find the ready money necessary to meet the cost of the journey. With Hatton's help he managed to raise a loan; but it was insufficient for his purpose and, in the end, he was obliged to pawn two of his most cherished possessions, which, indeed, he may have brought with him in case of such an emergency. One was his George, the costly badge worn by knights of the Garter; the other was the 'parliament jewel', presented to him more than ten years earlier by the English house of commons after his victory at Kilrush. As a result of this delay it was mid-December before he and the duke left Paris; and travelling in the depth of winter proved too much for the duke's health. By the time they reached Antwerp, at the end of the month, he was unfit to go any further; and there they were obliged to remain for some weeks.

Charles was concerned about his brother's illness, and sent his own doctor to attend him. But he was increasingly eager for Ormond's return. His friends in England were planning an insurrection. They believed that Cromwell had become so unpopular that the royalist cause would meet with little opposition; and they thought it essential that the king should be within easy reach, so that he could sail for England once they had got possession of a port where he could land. Charles himself was not very optimistic about this venture; but he knew that he must be ready to take any chance that might come, and he wanted to have Ormond at his side. Ormond was, therefore, summoned to Cologne; and on 14 February 1655 he and the king left the city secretly and travelled to Middleburg, on the coast of Holland. Here they remained in disguise, waiting for a call that never came: the royalist insurrection, mismanaged from the first, collapsed almost as soon as it began. It was some time before Charles and Ormond were aware how complete the failure had been; and they remained at Middleburg until the end of March. Ormond - ready, as he put it, 'to try for a hanging' - would have set off for England to get up-to-date news about the situation. But Charles would not allow him to take the risk; and they returned together to Cologne.

Ormond did not remain there for long. A few months later he was sent on a mission to the duke of Neuburg, a German prince closely allied to Spain. It was on Spanish military help that Charles now fixed his hopes; and Ormond's task was to persuade the duke to use his influence at Madrid on Charles's behalf. But the duke, though friendly, declared that his intervention would be useless; and it was not, in fact, until the following year, when Spain and England were at war, that the Spanish government showed any readiness to help Charles. But even then, though Charles was allowed to settle at Bruges in the Spanish Netherlands and was granted a pension, any decision about giving him direct military help was indefinitely postponed.

In the meantime, however, Charles was able, with Ormond's help, to show that even in exile he was not altogether without influence. When the French border fortress of Condé surrendered to the Spaniards in the summer of 1655 Ormond persuaded the officers of two Irish regiments, which had formed part of the garrison, to bring their men over to the king's service. Mazarin, fearful that other Irish regiments in the French service would follow this example, circulated among them a letter condemning this action and attacking both the king and Ormond. To this Ormond issued a reply, which seems to have had some effect, for other Irish troops subsequently left the French service when Charles called on them to do so. But there can be no doubt that Ormond's influence with their officers - who included many of his friends and relations - made them readier than they might otherwise have been to answer the king's call.

The outbreak of war between Spain and England, the king's settlement at Bruges and the readiness of Irish troops to quit the French service at his command all encouraged the hopes of the royalist exiles; and in the latter half of 1656 these hopes seemed brighter than they had been for a long time. But both the king and his advisers knew how much depended on the state of affairs in England. Even if the Spanish government could be persuaded to provide ships and men, nothing could be achieved unless the royalists in England could assemble a force strong enough to offer a real threat to the Cromwellian government and, above all, unless they could get control of a port where Charles and the troops he brought with him could safely land. But what was the likelihood that they could accomplish so much? Any decision must depend upon the answer to this question; and no clear answer could be given. Reports from England were frequent; but they were often vague and sometimes contradictory. Besides this, the Cromwellian secret service had penetrated some of the royalists groups, so that it was difficult to know whom to trust. The Spanish government, slow as always to make up its mind, would certainly not commit itself to active support without some firm assurance of effective royalist action in England. Month after month passed without any decision being reached; as 1657 neared its close the king's prospects seemed no brighter than they had been in the summer of the previous year.

It was in these circumstances that Ormond offered to go to England himself and get in touch with leading royalists there. If he found them prepared for immediate action he would join them. But, if not, he could at least bring back fuller and more reliable information than the king had so far had about the actual state of affairs. Hyde opposed this strongly: he thought Ormond's life too valuable to be risked on such a dangerous venture. But Ormond himself was still ready 'to try for a hanging'; and Charles, though he shared Hyde's fears, let him have his way.

(3)

Secrecy was absolutely essential to the success of Ormond's venture; but his absence would be noticed and must be accounted for: when he set out his ostensible business was another mission to the duke of Neuberg. He took with him as secretary Sir Richard Bellings, formerly a member of the Catholic Confederacy and one of those who had consistently stood by the treaties made with Ormond. Bellings knew nothing of the proposed visit to England; but he had to be told that the diplomatic mission was merely a blind. When Ormond left him at Cleves and turned back with no companion but one servant, the rest of the party continued on their way; and Bellings, in his dispatches to the king, maintained the fiction that Ormond was still with them - a necessary precaution lest the dispatches should fall into the wrong hands. This device achieved its purpose. On 13/23[1] January 1658 Lockhart, the English ambassador in Paris, reported to Thurloe that Ormond was on his way to the Imperial Diet; but on that day he was, in fact, in Antwerp, on his way to the Dutch coast, and waiting for the thousand guilders needed for his journey to England. A few days later he was in Holland; and here he was joined by an old acquaintance, Daniel O'Neill, Owen Roe's protestant nephew and one of the king's most trusted agents, who was also on a mission to England. There was some delay before they could hire a ship; but in the last week of January they landed at West March on the Sussex coast, a few miles from Colchester. Here they spent the night at an inn, where Ormond, finding no bed that he was willing to lie in, sat up all night, drinking warm ale to keep out the cold and playing shuffleboard with the locals.

Next day they moved on to Colchester; and from here Ormond sent his servant back to Bruges. At Chelmsford, their next stopping-place, he parted company with O'Neill and rode on to London, where he arrived on 30 January - a sombre day for such a devoted servant of Charles I. Here, according to his instructions, he first got in touch with Sir Philip Honeywood; and through him he met a considerable number of royalists, both among the citizens and among the country gentry. He was soon convinced that many of them were promising more than they could perform. Some were simply over-optimistic. Some wished to swell their own importance by exaggerating the number of men they could raise and the influence they could exercise. This was probably very much what Ormond had expected; what troubled him much more was to find that the royalists were divided among themselves. Different groups worked independently of each other, kept apart sometimes by personal jealousies, sometimes by differing views about the terms on which the king should be restored. He did not give up hope; but he was fully convinced that there was little prospect of a united and successful royalist insurrection unless the king himself should land with a strong military force.

The essential purpose of Ormond's visit had been to find out if the royalists were sufficiently strong and sufficiently well organized to

1. At this period the calendar in use in the British Isles was ten days behind that in use on the continent: 13 January in London was 23 January in Paris.

raise an insurrection that would present a real threat to the Cromwellian régime and, in particular, if they were in a position to seize and hold a port where the king might safely land with whatever troops he could raise on the continent. He was now convinced that there was little prospect of their being able to do either; and he was anxious to leave England as soon as possible. But he remained a week longer in the hope of receiving some message from Colonel Edward Popham, a leader of the presbyterian party; but when no message came he made his way to the coast and on 18/28 February he landed at Dieppe, 'after a dangerous and troublesome passage, in regard both of salt and fresh water', as he told Hyde in a letter written the next day.

Whatever the dangers Ormond met with in crossing the Channel, they were certainly not greater than the dangers to which he had been exposed in England. The government was constantly on the look-out for royalist agents; and any stranger might easily arouse suspicion. Besides this, there was always the possibility, especially in London, that Ormond would be recognized. He himself feared that his hair might betray him, for it was unusually light in colour - among the Irish he was known as 'the White Earl'. As a precaution, he wore a wig: but, finding this irksome, he decided to dye his hair black. Unfortunately, the dye he obtained for the purpose was ill-compounded: instead of turning his hair black it gave it a variety of colours and, in addition, scalded his scalp. Despite these dangers and misfortunes, 'Colonel Pickering', as he called himself, was able to go about his business. But he did so very cautiously. In London, he changed frequently from one lodging to another; he slept in his clothes, ready to move at a moment's notice; and he always made sure that there was an emergency exit, in case of sudden alarm. The most likely danger, however, was treachery; and against this it was difficult to guard. Cromwell had his agents among the royalist conspirators; and one of them, Sir Richard Willis, was among those whom Ormond met in London. It is not surprising, then, that Cromwell came to know of Ormond's presence. In a speech to the lord mayor, aldermen and common councillors of London, on 12 March, he warned them of the dangers to which the city and the whole country were exposed by 'the contrivements of Charles Stuart and his party both at home and abroad', and he emphasized the point by telling them that Ormond had been in London for three weeks and had 'departed privately' only three days earlier. If, as is likely, Cromwell was relying on information received from Willis, his error over the date is easily explained. Willis, though a traitor, was always careful not to put any man's life in danger; he would therefore hold back his information until he was sure that Ormond was safely out of the country and then assign a recent date in order to make his news appear the fresher.

A very different account of the affair became current at a later date. According to this, it was while Ormond was still in London that Cromwell was informed of his presence and thereupon sent Lord Broghill, later Earl of Orrery, to warn him that he would be arrested if he did not leave at once. There is nothing essentially improbable about this. As a prisoner, Ormond would be a constant centre of royalist conspiracy; and his execution would certainly be very unpopular. It might therefore seem wiser to let him go quietly. But the story rests solely on the not very reliable testimony of Orrery's chaplain, who records it in a biography of his patron, written many years later.

On the day after he landed at Dieppe, Ormond - although, as he wrote, 'so tired that I can hardly compose myself to make a dispatch' - sent Hyde a fairly detailed account of the information he had gained in England. The plans of the royalists were not so 'solidly projected' as he and Hyde had been led to believe; and he saw no probability of their being able to get possession of any city or town. But he was by no means hopeless. If the king could land at or near Yarmouth with the troops and supplies that he expected to get from the Spanish government, he would certainly be able to take the town 'and by that gain reputation and force sufficient to do (I think) his own business, and (I am sure) the king of Spain's'. Having described the situation in England as he had found it, he asks for the king's instructions about his own future movements. It is characteristic of Ormond's good nature that he ended his report by putting in a word for a Dr Quatermain, who had assisted him in his escape from England and who hoped to be appointed physician to the king.[1]

Some weeks passed before Ormond received a reply to this letter; and when it came almost the only cheerful item in it was that Dr Quatermain would be very welcome. For the rest, it was made up of complaints, which may have owed something of their sharpness to the fact that Hyde was recovering from a long fit of gout and was still

1. Dr Quatermain obtained the post he desired and retained it until his death in 1667.

in great pain. Ormond, he said, had left them 'very much in the dark'.
Messages from their friends in England had suggested hopeful moves
and combinations about which he had said nothing; and there were
potential supporters with whom he had made no contact. As for
Ormond's own future movements, they could offer no guidance,
since he had given them 'no more light to judge by'; and he himself
must tell them what he thinks fit to do. But after all this complaint,
the letter ends with a pious and friendly wish: 'God keep you, and
bring us well together'.

By the time this letter reached Ormond he was in Paris. The
establishment of an Anglo-French alliance had made France a
dangerous place for a royalist agent; but his sisters, Lady Clancarty
and Lady Hamilton, had found comparatively safe accommodation
for 'Mr Summers', as he now called himself, in the Feuillantine
convent where they resided. Not unnaturally, he read Hyde's letter,
as he said in reply, 'with very much admiration'. He had been sent to
England to find out if there was any prospect of a successful royalist
insurrection and, of so, to lead it. When he saw that there was no such
prospect, what could he do but return? He had found that there was
no assurance, or even probability, that the royalists could get possession
of a single town or fortress: 'how can you call this general positive
assertion no light, or suppose it did not comprehend all particulars
within my charge or view?' And he is amazed that Hyde should ask
him what he thinks fit to do with himself, 'that depending entirely
upon the king's orders and resolution'. Then, almost at the end, he
comes back to Hyde's implied criticism of what he had done, or
failed to do, during his stay in England: 'You could not think I had
time or madness enough about me to ravel all you have been weaving,
and new model [it] in ten or twelve days'.

Even before he had received this letter Hyde wrote again, and this
time in a less querulous tone. His main purpose was to convey the
king's desire that Ormond should join them as soon as possible. But
he adds at once, 'We dare not advise the way, which you will best
consider'. Ormond himself was well aware of the danger, for the
French authorities, warned by Cromwell, were on the look-out for
him; and the most direct route would probably be the most dangerous.
'I yet know not the way I shall get to you', he wrote in reply to Hyde,
'you may be sure it shall be as soon as I can; but it may be long first,
and consider that any way is nearer than by the Bastille'. To disarm
suspicion he rode south instead of north, and made first for Lyons,

which he reached in three days. From Lyons he went to Geneva, and then made his way through the Palatinate and down the Rhine. By this roundabout route he came safely to Brussels, where the king then was, in the second week of May.

(4)

Ormond found his friends in no very cheerful mood. Their hopes that Spain would provide naval and military support for a royalist descent upon England had been disappointed; and the Spanish pension, on which the king was largely dependent, had fallen so heavily in arrears that he could hardly maintain his household. But barely four months later their hopes were suddenly raised: on 7/17 September news of Cromwell's death reached Brussels. Almost three years earlier Ormond, writing to let Hyde know that he would rejoin him in a few days, had added a postscript to his letter: 'If Cromwell be not dead, see there bee a goode peece of beefe; if he be, chickins may serve'. Now Cromwell was dead; and the exiled royalists, whether they dined on beef or on chicken - or, as many of them must, on some humbler fare - were cheered by the news. But any expectation of speedy advantage to their cause was soon disappointed. Richard Cromwell succeeded his father without opposition; his title was recognized by foreign powers; and the fact that he held it by hereditary succession gave it an air of legitimacy. And even when this seeming stability proved illusory it was not at once apparent how, if at all, the conflict of parties could be turned to the king's advantage.

During these months, while royalists at home and abroad kept an anxious eye on the course of events, Ormond was much concerned about the affairs of his own family with which he had managed, despite all difficulties, to keep in touch. Very early in 1655 Lady Ormond had decided that it was time for their eldest son, Thomas - most commonly known by his courtesy title, Earl of Ossory - to see something of the world; and she intended that he should travel first to Italy and then to the Holy Land. By March all was ready for his departure. But at this point Penruddock's insurrection, though it collapsed almost at once, so startled the government that hundreds of known or suspected royalists throughout the country were arrested. Ossory, instead of going abroad, found himself in the Tower. Though no charge was ever brought against him, he did not recover his liberty for almost a year; and his health suffered so severely during his imprisonment that another six months passed before he was fit for foreign travel. By this time the idea of going to Italy and the Holy Land had been given up; and when he left England in August 1656 he went no farther than to Holland.

Before leaving England Ossory had been obliged to give an undertaking not to engage in any activity prejudicial to the Cromwellian regime; and for this reason he did not visit the king's court or mingle much with royalist exiles. But he soon made friends in Holland, among them Louis de Nassau, lord of Beverwaert, a natural son of Prince Maurice of Orange and governor of Sluys. With Beverwaert's daughter, Emilia, he fell deeply in love; and, as he told his father in a letter, 'I have reason to believe she has something of an esteem for me'. His own feelings he described in much more positive terms: he is, he says, 'so absolutely given over to this person that it is impossible for me ever to love any other'. Ormond, though he saw difficulties in the way, was quite ready to approve his son's choice. Lady Ormond was much more cautious. In particular, she was uneasy about the financial arrangements proposed by Beverwaert and which he refused to modify. He offered a dowry of £10,000, which Lady Ormond thought too little; and he insisted that Ossory should be provided with an annual income of £1,200, which she thought too much. On the latter point, at least, she had good reason to hesitate, for Ossory's income would have to be derived from the estate she had recovered in Ireland and which was all that she and her four other children had to depend on. The negotiations that followed took a long time, for everything had to be settled by correspondence; and since the commonwealth government had forbidden Lady Ormond to communicate with her husband, the exchange of letters between them was slow and uncertain. In the end, she was persuaded to let Ossory have his way; and, though she still thought the terms unsatisfactory, she gave her consent with a good grace. By the autumn of 1659 all the preliminaries had been settled; and it was arranged that the marriage should take place in November.

Ormond had not allowed family affairs to interfere with his service to the king; but for more than six months after Oliver Cromwell's death there was little that the royalists could do except wait on the course of events. The overthrow of the protectorate and the restoration of the Long Parliament in May 1659 revived their hopes; and these were strengthened by reports from their friends in England of plans for simultaneous risings in many parts of the country. In order to be within easy reach of England when the expected risings took place Charles left Brussels early in August and went to Calais, accompanied only by Ormond, Daniel O'Neill and Silius Titus, once a captain in the parliamentary army, but now an ardent royalist.

While they waited at Calais the king sent Ormond to Paris, partly to seek for support from the French government, but mainly to re-establish good relations between Charles and his mother, with whom he had for some time been on very uneasy terms. For this latter mission Ormond was hardly an appropriate choice: Henrietta Maria was unlikely to have forgotten or forgiven his intervention on behalf of the Duke of Gloucester eight years earlier. And on this occasion Ormond himself showed less than his usual discretion: when the queen declared that if she had been trusted the king would now be in England, his reply was that if she had not been trusted he would never have been out of England. It is hardly surprising that Hyde, when this was reported to him, told Ormond that he was not a good courtier.

Shortly after Ormond had rejoined the king, who had now moved to St Malo, came news of the collapse of the royalist insurrection in England. The king, always hopeful, now reverted to an earlier plan and decided to seek help from France and Spain. The two countries had been long at war; but their plenipotentiaries were now meeting at Fuentarabia, in the Pyrenees, to arrange terms of peace; and Charles decided to go there himself and enlist their joint support. He travelled slowly, however, and it was October before he and his companions reached Toulouse. Here they were told that the peace conference had already ended. So Ormond was left at Toulouse, in order that he might meet Mazarin when he arrived there on his way back to Paris; and the king, with the rest of the small party, rode on to visit the Spanish minister, Don Luis de Haro. While he waited at Toulouse Ormond wrote to Sir Edward Nicholas, one of the king's secretaries, who was then in Brussels:

> I live in a retiredness more suitable to my fortune than wholesome for my spleen, yet I thank God I am in perfect health... We wanderers have the divertisement of seeing new places to refresh the melancholy of our spirits, and we are not subject to the complaints and sights of our friends in misery.

Ormond was not left to enjoy either his solitude or the sights of Toulouse for long. Within a few days he discovered that the news they had been given was false and that the peace conference was still in progress; so he set off once more and joined the king at Fuentarabia.

Here he found Charles in a cheerful mood, for the Spanish minister had received him with royal honours and seemed disposed to give some substantial support to his cause. Mazarin, however, had been much more cautious. He had sent friendly messages; but, with many specious excuses, he had declined to meet the king. But he did agree to have a discussion with Ormond, though he insisted that this should be so arranged as to have the appearance of an accidental encounter.[1] Mazarin listened politely while Ormond presented his master's case and indicated the advantages that France would gain by contributing to his restoration; but while he expressed sympathy with Charles, he made it quite clear that he could not, in the present circumstances, provide the help that Ormond sought. All the comfort he offered was that if circumstances were to change France might be free to follow a different policy. Ormond had his meeting with Mazarin on 12 November. Next day Charles and his companions set off on their return journey; and though they had, in fact, little more reason to expect active help from either Spain or France than when they arrived, Charles, optimistic as always, was in a cheerful mood. It was as they jogged along through the flat Gascon landscape that Ormond's eldest son, in far away Holland, was married to his Emilia, with none of his family, save one brother, to keep him company. But the marriage proved a happy one. And, though they could not know this at the time, within six months the king would come to his own and their world would be transformed.

---

1. Ormond seems to have had no difficulty in conversing in French; but he admits that he found it very difficult indeed to write a letter in French.

CHAPTER VI

The Restoration

(1)

As Charles and Ormond made their way slowly back to Brussels their hopes were still fixed on a royalist expedition to England; and despite Mazarin's refusal to commit himself they still looked to France for financial and military support. At Colombes, not far from Paris, they lingered for a week, while Charles re-established good relations with his mother, from whom he had been for some time estranged, and Ormond prepared a memorandum that would, they hoped, remove Mazarin's doubts and induce him to provide the help they wanted. But Mazarin was not to be persuaded; and when the travellers eventually reached Brussels, late in December, the king's propsects seemed no brighter than when they had set out almost five months earlier.

Already, however, the situation in England was changing. Ormond had assured Mazarin, in a memorandum drawn up on 10 December, that 'his majesty hath no reason to despair of his speedy restoration, even by his subjects solely'; and though one may reasonably suppose that he put this forward as a means of winning French support rather than as an indication of what he himself expected, the way was, in fact, being prepared for the king's peaceful return to England.

The army, which had restored the rump of the Long Parliament in May, had expelled it once more in October. But George Monck, commander of the forces in Scotland, was determined to intervene on its behalf. He was not a man to move hastily; but by the end of the year, having secured his position in Scotland and purged his army of officers on whom he could not rely, he was ready to act. On 2 January 1660 he crossed the Tweed and began a slow march southward. He met with no opposition, for the English commanders - Fleetwood, Lambert and Desborough - could not trust their troops. They were, indeed, so uncertain of their own authority that they had already allowed the parliament to re-assemble. But by this time all attention was fixed on Monck himself. It was clear now that the future of the country lay in his hands; though what his intentions might be no one knew.

Royalists, both at home and abroad, watched these developments eagerly; and many of them were ready to regard Monck as the destined restorer of the monarchy. But Ormond, despite the hopeful opinion he had expressed to Mazarin, took a more cautious view. In a letter to Lord Jermyn he expressed the belief that Monck would go beyond his declared purpose of supporting the parliament; but, he added, 'what his further intentions are, or for whom, I will not so much as guess'. He thought that the royalists in general were too optimistic: '...all of our side write as if they were pleased with the face of things, but I see no particulars that warrant so much satisfaction'. This was written towards the end of January, at a time when royalist hopes were rising, in Ireland as well as in England; but Ormond's caution was natural enough in one who had so often been disappointed. It was not, in fact, until six weeks later that a decisive step towards the restoration of monarchy was taken. In mid-March, when the Long Parliament had dissolved itself after arranging for new elections, Monck at last, and in the utmost secrecy, committed himself to the royalist cause.

From this point onward all went smoothly. On 25 April the newly-elected members took their seats at Westminster. A small group of peers met in their own chamber and re-established, after an interval of more than ten years, a house of lords. On 1 May both houses received, with proper respect, letters addressed to them by the king; and they agreed in a declaration that, according to the fundamental laws of the kingdom, government was and ought to be by king, lords and commons. A week later King Charles II was proclaimed in London, with all the traditional ceremony; and on 25 May he landed at Dover. Among those who accompanied him were Ormond and two of his sons, Ossory and Richard.

(2)

The restoration marked the opening of a new phase in Ormond's career. Now, for the first time, he was at the centre of power. As lord lieutenant of Ireland he had struggled against great odds to re-establish the king's authority; but he had never been in a position to exercise direct and continuous influence on royal policy, however much it might affect Irish affairs. During the exile he had been in the innermost counsels of the king, but of a king without a kingdom. Now, when Charles was king in fact as well as in name, Ormond was one of the advisers on whom he mainly relied; and though his influence on royal policy soon declined, he could never, while Charles lived, be wholly ignored by rival politicians struggling to keep or gain power. Ormond's career, down to the end of the 1640s, belongs primarily to the history of Ireland; from the Restoration onward it belongs to the history of the monarchy as a whole.

The numerous titles and offices that the king now conferred upon him reflect not only gratitude for the past but also continued dependence on his services. He was appointed Lord Steward of the Household, a post that carried with it both patronage and profit, High Steward of Westminster, of Kingston and of Bristol, and lord lieutenant of Somerset. He was created Earl of Brecknock in the peerage of England, and so became a member of the English house of lords. He was sworn of the English privy council, where he, along with Hyde, now Earl of Clarendon, and three or four others formed a kind of inner cabinet that advised the king on all aspects of policy. At Charles's coronation, on 23 April 1661, he held the office of Lord High Steward of England, and in that capacity he carried St Edward's Crown before the king. Never before had an Irishman attained such high rank among the aristocracy of England. Besides all this, his advancement to the dukedom of Ormond, on 30 March 1661, gave him a unique place in the peerage of his own country.

The Restoration brought to Ormond not only these signal marks of royal favour but also immediate relief from the burden of poverty he had borne for so many years. No longer need he go in threadbare clothes, or walk while others rode in their coaches. A man who stood so high as he did in the king's favour could easily command credit; and, within a very short time, the recovery of his estates assured him of a regular income. In this respect he was better off than hundreds of other Irish proprietors whose lands, like his, had been confiscated by the Commonwealth government and parcelled out among its own supporters. They were kept waiting while attempts were made to devise a compromise that would satisfy the just claims of the dispossessed without dangerously alienating the new proprietors; but Ormond was quickly restored to full possession of all he had held at the outbreak of the insurrection in 1641. Indeed, in one respect he recovered more than he had lost; for the palatine rights in County

Tipperary, formerly enjoyed by the Ormonds but confiscated by James I, were now restored by Charles II.

With this full restoration of his estates Ormond might seem to be put in a comfortable financial position. In fact, for the rest of his life he was never wholly free from some measure of anxiety over money; and this despite the fact that for more than half the period between the Restoration and his death he held the lucrative office of lord lieutenant of Ireland. This failure to live within his means did not arise from thoughtless self-indulgence. Unlike so many of his contemporaries, he kept no mistresses. Though he sometimes lost considerable sums at cards during his attendance at court, he was not an habitual gambler. His personal tastes were simple - a boiled leg of mutton was his favourite dish at dinner. But he was convinced that a great nobleman should maintain a great household. The head of the Butler family could not live like a private gentleman, even when he was out of office. Quite apart from the troop of servants, upper and lower, employed in the gardens, the stables and the house, he regularly maintained ten, and sometimes as many as twenty, gentlemen of good family, who formed a kind of miniature court in which he and his duchess were the central figures. As lord lieutenant of Ireland he felt it his duty to live with a magnificence worthy of the king whom he represented; and the revenues of the post, great as they were, fell short of his expenditure. When it is remembered that, besides all this, Ormond had to provide for his three sons, it will seem less surprising than might appear at first sight that he died, as he had lived, in debt. And it is characteristic of the man that when he lay on his deathbed the aspect of his indebtedness that seemed to trouble him most was that he could not make adequate provision for his servants.

In the cheerful spring of 1660 it is unlikely that Ormond's thoughts ran on the gloomy topics of debt and death. Besides his share in the public jubilation over the king's return he had the private joy of reunion with his family, from whom he had so long been separated. He and his wife had not been together since August 1651, when Lady Ormond left Caen in order to obtain from the authorities in London some provision for herself and her children; and during this long interval communication between them had been infrequent and precarious. Lady Ormond refers to the hardship of their long separation in a letter to her husband written on 11 May 1660, after the news of the king's return had reached her at Dunmore:

I beleve it will seme strange to you to reserve an avowede
address from mee, whose misfortune has bene such, as
besides your absence, *it was made penalle for mee to reseve
letters*.

So great is her excitement at the prospect of their reunion that she can
hardly express herself coherently - 'I suspect myselfe', she says, 'not
to write sense' - but her affection for her husband comes through
clearly. Though she looks forward to kissing the king's hand, 'which
I shall endeavour with all the speede I cane, as what I covete beyonde
all things in this world', she adds at once, 'next that of seeinge you,
such exceptions I know to be less a compliment, but more of truth,
and in that respect beter'.

Eager though Lady Ormond was to join her husband, preparations
for the journey took time; and it was June before she and her daughters,
Elizabeth and Mary, arrived in London. Ossory and Richard, like
Ormond himself, had come over from Holland with the king and the
Duke of York; and the youngest son, John, arrived somewhat later.
For the first time in almost a decade the whole family was together.

When this reunion took place Ormond's children, of whom he had
seen so little for many years, were children no longer. Ossory was
already married; and Lady Ormond insisted, no doubt wisely, that he
and his wife should have an establishment of their own. He was a
close friend of the Duke of York - he was one of the two witnesses at
the duke's secret marriage to Anne Hyde on 3 September 1660 - and
this association assured his advancement in the royal service. Richard
came of age a few months after the Restoration; and in the following
year he was raised to the peerage as Earl of Arran. John, at seventeen,
was almost old enough to enter on the career of debauchery and
drunkenness that led to his early death sixteen years later.[1] Both the
daughters were now of marriageable age; and Lady Ormond soon
found them husbands of suitable rank and fortune. Within a few
months Elizabeth was married to Philip Stanhope, second Earl of
Chesterfield; and negotiations were soon in train for a match between

---

1. Ormond had had five other sons, who had died in infancy. Of these, the first
had been christened Thomas, after the tenth earl ('Black Tom'), for whom
Ormond had a great admiration; the name was then given to the second son,
later Earl of Ossory. Of the others who died in infancy, three had been
christened James, after their father. The name was revived in the next
generation: Ossory's son and heir (afterwards second Duke of Ormond) was
christened James.

Mary and William, Lord Cavendish, afterwards first Duke of Devonshire. Before they were completed, however, Ormond had returned to Ireland as lord lieutenant; and it was at Kilkenny that the couple were married, in October 1662.

(3)

Throughout the whole period of the exile Ormond had remained, in title, lord lieutenant of Ireland. But it is very unlikely that he wished to resume the duties of the office; and there is nothing to suggest that he felt in any way aggrieved when George Monck, now Duke of Albemarle, was, at his own request, appointed lord lieutenant in his place a few weeks after the king's return. At this time Ormond's future career seemed to lie in England rather than in Ireland. Among the king's principal advisers his influence was second only to that of Sir Edward Hyde - now Earl of Clarendon; and he and Clarendon were close friends and allies. Ormond was not selfishly ambitious and was always ready to serve the king in whatever capacity the king himself might choose; but it was natural that he should prefer to be at the centre of power rather than to exercise vice-regal authority in a subordinate kingdom, where he must always act in accordance with the instructions that he received.

Ormond's regular attendance upon the king made it necessary for him to live within easy reach of the court; and he took a house in Chelsea. But here he had little opportunity to enjoy the open-air exercise that he loved and that he considered essential to his health; and in 1661 he purchased Moor Park, in Hertfordshire,[1] where he could easily go in 'such starts of retirement' - to use his own phrase - as his duties allowed him. The house itself was comparatively small; but the gardens were excellent, 'full of delightful walks and fountains and terraces with covered walks for rainy weather'; and the park was well-wooded and stocked with deer. He was not able to make as much use of Moor Park as he had expected, for in the following year he was obliged to return to Ireland. But his correspondence with James Buck, whom he left in charge, shows how keenly he was interested in improving the grounds.

Though Ormond was no longer lord lieutenant he was still ready to

1. Not to be confused with Sir William Temple's house of the same name in Surrey.

78

use his influence in Irish affairs; and in the summer of 1660 he was much concerned about the state of the Church of Ireland. It had suffered so heavily at the hands both of Confederates and Cromwellians that it could hardly be said to have survived as an organized body: at the time of the Restoration sixteen bishoprics - two thirds of the whole number - were vacant. It was due very largely to Ormond's influence that the king, in August 1660, made nominations to all but one of these vacancies. Since at that time no appointments had yet been made to the numerous episcopal vacancies in England, this was the first unmistakable indication that the restoration of the monarchy was to involve the restoration of the church also.

The restoration of episcopacy aroused some resentment among the presbyterians in Ulster; but the Roman Catholics, who knew that the best they could hope for so far as religion was concerned was freedom from persecution, were much more anxious about the settlement of landed property. The Cromwellian conquest had been followed by an extensive confiscation of estates; and though this affected every proprietor who could not prove his 'constant good affection to the Commonwealth of England', it was the Catholic landlords who had suffered most heavily. Some of the confiscated land had been granted to Cromwellian soldiers in lieu of arrears of pay, some to those who had advanced money for the suppression of the insurrection of 1641, some to leading parliamentarians; and some remained in the hands of the government. Now that the monarchy was restored those who had lost their estates hoped to recover them, while those in possession of confiscated land were determined to retain what they held.

In the early summer of 1660 the two rival groups had their agents in London; and Ormond could hardly avoid becoming involved, for the dispossessed Catholics looked to him to support their claims under the treaties of 1646 and 1649. Though he felt that the conduct of the Catholics themselves had released him from any obligation under these treaties, Ormond was willing to give them such help as he could. His advice was that they should proceed cautiously, appealing to the king's generosity rather than vaunting their own merits. But the Catholic agents rejected this advice. Instead, they turned to Richard Talbot,[1] a member of the Duke of York's household, who had at one time served in the Confederate army. It proved an unfortunate choice. Talbot's influence was much less than they had supposed; his judgement was not to be relied upon; and he was a

1. Later Duke of Tyrconnell.

79

bitter enemy of Ormond, whom he constantly abused, both in public and private. On one occasion he went so far that Ormond complained to the king, and asked if it was his majesty's pleasure 'that at this time of day he should put off his doublet and fight duels with Dick Talbot'. It is hardly surprising, then, that he left the Catholic agents to follow the policy that they had themselves chosen; and though he was still ready to use his influence on behalf of individual claimants whom he thought worthy of support, he felt himself free from any obligation to the dispossessed Catholics in general. But, despite his desire to stand aside, he soon found that he could not avoid being deeply involved in the conflict over landed property in Ireland, which was to continue throughout the rest of his life and to have a powerful influence on his career.

The king was willing to do what he could for the Catholic claimants, and especially for those of them who had served him abroad during the interregnum; but he knew that any threat to the position of the Cromwellian settlers would arouse dangerous discontent, not only in Ireland but in England. In these circumstances he gladly accepted a proposal put forward by Roger Boyle, Earl of Orrery, an astute politician who had changed sides more than once during the previous decade but had ended up as a royalist and had been rewarded with an earldom at the Restoration. His proposal was based on the fact that not all the land confiscated by the Commonwealth government had so far been disposed of; and what remained was now in the king's hands. According to Orrery, this land was sufficient to enable the king to satisfy all legitimate claims: if a dispossessed proprietor could establish his right to recover his estate, now in the possession of a Cromwellian settler, he might safely be restored; for the Cromwellian could be compensated by the grant of an estate of equal value out of the lands at the king's disposal.

Orrery's purpose was probably to keep the rival parties quiet until the king's authority had been so firmly established that he could impose his will on both, for he was too well informed to be deceived by his own fallacious calculations. Ormond, equally well informed and much more honest, exposed the weakness of the scheme in a single sentence: 'There must be new discoveries made of a new Ireland, for the old will not serve to satisfy these engagements'.

Orrery's proposal, having been approved by the king, was embodied in a Royal Declaration, issued in November 1660; and commissioners were appointed to execute its provisions. But though the commissioners heard claims and, where they found in favour of the claimant, issued a decree for his restoration, their decrees had no effect; for since they lacked statutory authority the courts refused to enforce them. The king had hoped to postpone the calling of an Irish parliament until the controversial land question was safely out of the way. But now he could delay no longer: both the economic and the political condition of Ireland would remain precarious until property rights had been established on a secure basis; and since it was clear that only an act of parliament could provide that security a parliament must be held.

This decision had important consequences for Ormond. The king was convinced that while the Irish parliament was in session there should be a resident lord lieutenant; but Albemarle, who had hitherto held the office as an absentee, was still unwilling to go to Ireland and suggested that Ormond should take his place. To this the king agreed; and Ormond, though he would much rather have remained in London, was true to his principle of serving the king in whatever capacity the king himself might choose, and accepted the post. Clarendon was not present when this decision was taken; but as soon as he heard of it he scolded Ormond, in the king's presence, for his folly in undertaking the government of Ireland; and, at least by implication, he blamed the king for having asked him to do so.

Ormond's own attitude appears very clearly in a letter to a friend, written in November 1661, shortly after the king's decision to appoint him lord lieutenant had been announced in council:

> In that emloyment, besides many other unpleasant difficulties, there are two disadvantages proper to me; one of the contending parties believing I owe them more kindness and protection, than I can find myself chargeable with; and the other suspecting I retain that prejudice to them, which I am as free from.

This proved to be an accurate forecast of the position in which he soon found himself. Among the dispossessed Catholics he was regarded as one who had deserted his true friends and faithful allies; and to the more militant of the Cromwellian settlers he seemed an enemy of the English and protestant interest in Ireland. But Ormond did not allow himself to be troubled by such accusations and suspicions. He had foreseen from the beginning that it would be impossible to devise any settlement of landed property that would satisfy all conflicting claims; and he was content to do what he could, within the very narrow limits imposed by the instructions he received from England, to promote the welfare of all the people of Ireland.

Though the decision to send Ormond to Ireland as lord lieutenant was taken in November 1661, the formal appointment was not made until the following February; and for some months after that his duties at court kept him in England. As lord steward of the household it was his responsibility to make preparations for the reception of the king's bride, Catherine of Braganza; and after her landing at Plymouth, in May, she had to be escorted to London and established in the apartments provided for her. In the end, it was not until 8 July that he was free to set off for Chester, then the usual port of embarcation for travellers to Dublin.

A viceroy of Ireland, on his way to take up his duties, was normally accompanied by a large body of attendants; and this was a practice from which Ormond, who felt it his duty to maintain all the state befitting one who represented the king, was unlikely to depart. But on this occasion his train was further swollen by a large number of Irish nobles and gentlemen who had come to London to protect their interests in the impending settlement of estates and who now returned home in Ormond's company. It is not surprising that John Evelyn, who was a close friend of Ossory and had come to take leave of the duke and duchess, was impressed by the size of the 'extraordinary retinue' with which they set off.

The long string of coaches, accompanied by scores of outriders, travelled slowly; and progress was further delayed by the ceremonial inseparable from such a journey: in every county that they passed through they must pause while the militia paraded and the lord lieutenant of the county paid his respects to Ormond. Two weeks had passed before they reached Chester; and when they got there they found the weather so stormy and the wind so unfavourable that it was thought best to continue their journey to Holyhead and take ship there. But at Holyhead the storm was still raging; and it was only after a difficult and dangerous passage that the duke and duchess landed at Howth, on Saturday, 26 July. It was a little more than eleven and a half years earlier that Ormond had left Ireland on an even longer and stormier voyage into exile.

CHAPTER VII

Ormond's Viceroyalty, 1662-1669

(1)

In all but the unruliness of the sea Ormond's return to Ireland was very different from his departure in December 1650. Then he had been driven out with abuse; now he was received with acclamation. At Howth, where he spent the Saturday night, the peasantry welcomed him with dances, flowers and Gaelic songs. On Sunday he rode into Dublin, the central figure in a long procession of coaches and cavalry, through streets lined by cheering crowds, to be formally sworn in as lord lieutenant. Next day the ceremony of welcome continued, with the presentation of addresses by both houses of parliament, the clergy, the university and the city; while the common people, enlivened by a generous distribution of wine, celebrated the occasion with dancing and bell-ringing.

For almost seven years after his arrival in Dublin Ormond remained at the head of the Irish administration; and it was natural that people on both sides of the channel - and especially those who were dissatisfied with the policy followed - should regard him as responsible for the state of the country under his government. But his freedom of action was, in fact, narrowly limited. On all matters of importance the action to be taken in Ireland was decided in England, where there was a committee of council for Irish affairs; and Ormond, whatever his own opinion might be, was obliged to act in accordance with the instructions he received. The character of these instructions seldom reflected any concern for the welfare of Ireland, except in so far as it might be of benefit to England, and was sometimes influenced by the selfish personal interests of English politicians. Throughout the greater part of the viceroyalty there was a struggle for power between rival groups at court; and those who were seeking to overthrow Clarendon were always ready to embarrass his friend and ally Ormond. It is true that Ormond could, and sometimes did, apply directly to the king for support; but Charles, though he had a genuine regard for him, was not a man on whom it was safe to rely; and Ormond's

83

efforts to improve the Irish economy were liable to be frustrated by the selfishness of English courtiers. Public opinion regarded him as responsible for the policies he followed and some historians have done the same; but on every issue of importance the final decision was taken in London, not in Dublin; and the well-being of Ireland was rarely, if ever, the major consideration.

(2)

Ormond had been appointed lord lieutenant in Monck's place because it was considered desirable that Ireland should have a resident lord lieutenant during the meeting of parliament. But his duties at court had delayed his departure so long that he did not reach Dublin until well over a year after parliament had met. Its composition reflected the change in the distribution of property and influence that had taken place during the previous decade. Both in the county constituencies and in those cities and boroughs that returned members to parliament protestant influence was now dominant; and the elections, in May 1661, had returned a wholly protestant house of commons. In the house of lords a few Roman Catholic peers took their seats, but they could exercise little or no influence. The main purpose for which this parliament had been called was to pass a measure giving statutory authority to the Royal Declaration of 30 November 1660; and had it been free to act as it chose it is very unlikely that it would have done so. But the powers of the Irish parliament were narrowly limited: it could accept or reject, but could not amend, bills approved in advance by the Irish and English councils.[1] It must, therefore, choose between accepting as it stood the bill presented to it (commonly called the Bill of Settlement) or else face an indefinite period of conflict over rival claims to landed property. After long and angry debate parliament passed the bill; and it was among those to which Ormond signified the royal assent shortly after his arrival. But parliament did not regard this as a final measure and demanded that an amending bill should be prepared.

It was not long before the anxiety expressed in parliament, and especially in the house of commons, was shown to have some

1. This was the effect of a statute passed by the Irish parliament in 1494, generally called Poynings' Law, after the lord deputy at the time, Sir Edward Poynings.

justification. The commissioners appointed by the crown to administer the act formed a court of claims, before which any dispossessed proprietor seeking to prove that he was entitled to recover his estate could present his case; and such a large majority of those who did so were successful that it soon became clear that the land at the disposal of the crown would be insufficient to compensate more than a small fraction of those Cromwellians who were now threatened with the loss of their newly-acquired property. Though the decrees issued by the court of claims did not lead to any immediate transfer of property, there was widespread alarm among the new settlers. Ormond did what he could to reassure them; but he himself was very uneasy about the situation. If, as he feared might happen, there was a Cromwellian insurrection he was ill-prepared to deal with it. The army was not a coherent body: troops of horse and companies of foot were billeted here and there throughout the country; and, since the treasury was empty, he could not meet the cost of assembling any considerable force. Besides this, the army was that inherited from the Commonwealth, only partially purged of the more irreconcilable elements; and how it would behave in such a crisis as he feared might arise was very doubtful. The only body of troops on which he could safely depend was the newly-formed regiment of guards, twelve hundred strong, which he had himself enlisted in England.

He described the state of affairs in a report to the king, on 7 February 1663, and made an urgent plea for financial assistance that would enable him to draw together a considerable part of the army and keep it on an active service footing. It is clear that he regarded this as a precautionary measure and still hoped that the widespread discontent among the Cromwellian settlers would pass away without any violent upheaval. But already, when he wrote this report, a conspiracy had been formed that was to put both the authority of the government and his own life in danger.

(3)

The leading figure among the conspirators was Thomas Blood, whose later career was to make him one of the most notorious characters in the Restoration period. Blood regarded Ormond with deep and enduring hatred, for he held him responsible for the act of settlement, by which, or so he claimed, he had been deprived of an estate that was rightfully his. The other conspirators, though they did not share his hatred of Ormond, were equally determined that the Cromwellian settlers should retain their property intact. Their plan was to strike at the centre of power by seizing Dublin Castle and taking Ormond prisoner. This was to be the signal for the army, which they believed would support them, to secure all the principal cities and towns throughout the kingdom; and the way would then be open, or so they hoped, for the re-establishment of the Commonwealth.

This daring scheme might have had at least initial success but for the fact that the conspirators had among them an informer who let Ormond know, through an intermediary, what was being planned. The information he sent was, however, incomplete; and it did not always reach Ormond promptly: he had barely twenty-four hours' notice of a plan to seize Dublin Castle on 5 March 1663. The precautions he immediately took were sufficient to frighten off the plotters; but they managed to avoid arrest and they were fully determined to try again.

This abortive attempt seems to have convinced Ormond that the danger was greater than he had supposed; and he set to work to gather all the information that he could about the conspiracy. His aim was not to force the conspirators to abandon their design, but to catch them in the act. He might, had he chosen, have arrested at least some of them; and he explains his reason for not doing so in a report to the king on 16 May:

> That which hath prevailed upon me against the reasons which might induce a more early disappointment of the design are principally that I have and shall have very good and hourly information of their transactions, and it is doubtful whether the intention and contrivance of what they are about without some overt act will by our law be capitally penal. If not, then would these bold machinations go unpunished and consequently your government would never be free from them.

Ormond admits that his policy of leaving the conspirators at liberty in the hope of catching them red-handed was a dangerous one. But since he himself was their intended victim he had the strongest possible inducement to lay his plans carefully: 'I govern myself by the best reason I have, the rather that I am to answer the misguiding of that at the price of my life'.

Ormond wrote this report on a Saturday; and early in the following week the conspirators were assembled in Dublin, ready for another attempt to seize the Castle. According to an account later provided by one of them, they had a long argument about how Ormond was to be treated. Some thought he should be killed; others opposed this, saying that he had always been 'a great patron to the English and protestant religion'. The dispute was not settled until the day before the attempt was to be made; and then the decision went against Ormond, on the ground that 'he was so firm to the crown that they could not be safe, let their success be never so good, for by his interest in the kingdom and army one time or other he would prevail against them'.

On Wednesday, 20 May, while the conspirators were still debating whether or not he should be killed, Ormond received warning of their design, which was to be put into execution early on Thursday morning. He at once took all necessary precautions; and the stratagem by which they hoped to get possession of the Castle would have failed had it been attempted. But, in the meantime, the conspirators themselves had become alarmed; and at about nine o'clock on Wednesday evening they had decided to postpone action and disperse. News of their change of plan did not reach Ormond until several hours later; and although he at once sent out parties to arrest the conspirators, several of them had escaped in the interval. Among those who did so the most important was Thomas Blood. Though he had been foiled on this occasion, his determination to take Ormond's life remained as strong as ever; and seven years later he was to make another and even more daring attempt.

Ormond had feared that the conspirators would escape execution unless they could be proved to have committed some overt act against the king. Now, however, his doubts were set at rest. Four of the prisoners were put on trial for high treason, found guilty and hanged. Ormond was neither bloodthirsty nor revengeful; but he was convinced that in the uneasy state of the country it was necessary to assert the government's authority; and, having done so, he was satisfied. The remaining prisoners were kept for a time in captivity; but there were no more executions.

(4)

Ormond's successful handling of the Castle plot certainly strengthened his authority; and the danger of a Cromwellian insurrection was, at least for the time being, removed. But the urgent problem of establishing the tenure of landed property on some firm basis remained as far as ever from solution. Ormond himself cannot have had much faith in the act of settlement, based as it was on Orrery's fallacious calculation of the amount of land available; but hitherto he had kept his doubts to himself. Now he was ready to declare openly that it could not, in its existing form, be made to work. On 20 June, when the excitement aroused by the Castle plot had barely died down, he wrote to Sir Henry Bennet,[1] the secretary of state with responsibility for Irish affairs:

> I am persuaded no good settlement will ever be brought to
> pass by the act so called unless some other act, which may
> be called explanatory, but must in effect be an alteration, be
> superadded. And this is the opinion of all the best and
> soberest persons concerned, English and Irish.

Within a few weeks Ormond and his advisers were at work on the preparation of an explanatory measure. It proved a difficult business, which left him little time for rest and, what was worse, none at all for exercise, which, as he complained to Bennet, 'is as necessary to me as sleep'. It was presumably this confinement within doors that brought on 'the extraordinary indisposition of the spleen' from which he suffered in July. Nevertheless, he stuck to the task; and by September the bill was completed and sent to England for consideration by the English council. In the dispatch that accompanied the bill Ormond urged that it should be returned as speedily as possible. But the transmission of the bill to England proved to be only the beginning of a long and difficult process; and more than two years were to elapse before the bill, in a much altered form, was passed into law.

The issues involved in these lengthy negotiations are clearly set out by Ormond in a letter to his old friend Clarendon:

> It is most evident that a settlement one way or another is
> absolutely necessary, and that till there be one, there can be
> neither security nor improvement in this kingdom. And if
> you look upon the composition of this council and parliament
> you will not think it probable it can be with much favour, or
> indeed reasonable regard, to the Irish. If it be, it will not
> pass; and if it be not, we must look for all the clamour that
> can be raised by undone men.

It is clear enough from this passage that Ormond was not unsympathetic to the dispossessed Roman Catholics, among whom,

1. Raised to the peerage (Lord Arlington), 1663.

indeed, were many of his own close relations; but it is equally clear that he did not think it possible to get through parliament any measure that would do justice to their claims. The bill he had sent to England had been drawn up with these considerations in mind; and it did as much for the dispossessed Catholics as he thought the house of commons might be induced to accept.

From this time onwards things went much more slowly than Ormond had hoped. The English council, when it began to consider the bill after many weeks' delay, regarded it as over-generous to the Cromwellian settlers and proposed changes that would substantially reduce the area allotted to them. Ormond assured Bennet, in a letter of 16 November, that if the bill were altered in the way proposed 'it will not pass in this parliament'. His warning seems to have had little effect; and six weeks later, on 29 December, he sent a long memorandum on the subject to the king. In substance, it came to this: if the changes in the explanatory bill were so unfavourable to the Cromwellian interest that parliament rejected it, then the settlement of landed property would have to be made on the authority of the crown alone and would have to be supported by military force; in these circumstances the Irish army could not be depended upon and troops would have to be sent from England. Ormond may have feared, on reflection, that this memorandum might give the impression that he was advising the king to impose by military force a settlement rejected by the Irish parliament; and a week later he wrote to him again. Though he does not withdraw anything he had said in the memorandum, there is a marked change of emphasis. He is now hopeful that when parliament re-assembles it will be in a co-operative mood, so that the extraordinary measures referred to in the memorandum will not be required. And with regard to those measures he ends on a note of caution. If the king should be obliged to send an army from England to impose a land settlement he must remember that it is made up of Englishmen, 'who will not willingly be thought to countenance the oppression of the worst English in favour of the best Irish'.

When this letter was written, early in January 1664, the English council had made little progress on the revision of the explanatory bill; and it was not until April that it had prepared a substantial number of amendments. Up to this point there had been no consultation with Ormond; but now the king directed that the amendments so far proposed should be sent to him for his opinion. Before they arrived, however, Ormond had asked for and received the king's permission to go to London, so that he could exercise a direct influence in giving the bill the form in which it would eventually be presented to parliament. Late in May he set sail from Dublin. leaving his eldest son, Ossory, as lord deputy. But even after Ormond's arrival in London the business still dragged, partly because so many individuals, including English courtiers who had received from the king grants of forfeited land, wished to have special clauses inserted in their favour. It was not until the summer of 1665 that the bill at last received its final form; and it was not until the December of that year that it was passed, after long and stormy debate, by the Irish parliament.

Ormond had been almost continuously involved in the preparation of the bill from the time of its inception; and it was very largely due to his influence that the Irish parliament was induced to pass it. A contemporary, Sir Winston Churchill, describes the strength and fury of the opposition, and then continues:

> neither was it in the power of any man's single reputation
> but the duke's only to have kept it from sinking; who by an
> eloquence (peculiar to himself) seemingly unconcerned,
> but certainly extemporary, so charmed their fears and
> jealousies that they that were most displeased with the bill
> were yet so pleased with the overtures he had made them
> that when it came to pass it had only one negative.

Though Ormond was so closely concerned both in the preparation of the bill and in securing its passage through parliament, its character was determined by circumstances beyond his control. But it was natural that the dispossessed Irish, forgetting how very imperfectly they had kept the terms of the treaties they had made with him, should hold him responsible for their failure to recover more than a small fraction of what they had lost. To them he was, and remained, what Bishop Nicholas French called him, 'The unkind desertor of loyall men and true frinds'.[1]

(5)

The revision of the explanatory bill, though it detained Ormond in England for well over a year, did not occupy the whole of his time; and during this period he had more leisure from public business than

1. This was the title of a pamphlet by French, published in 1676.

while he was at the head of the government in Dublin. When he received the king's permission to go to London he had taken a house in Chelsea; and the duchess, who always kept a sharp eye on household affairs, had gone there in advance so that all should be in order when the duke arrived. At Chelsea he was within easy reach of the court, where his presence was often required; and Moor Park, his country house - of which he had so far seen so little - was near enough for him to be able to retire there from time to time.

While the Ormonds were in England two family events gave cause for rejoicing. In September 1664 their second son, Richard, Earl of Arran, married Lady Mary Stewart. This was a match of which the duchess, who had been so uneasy about Ossory's choice of a wife, could be perfectly satisfied. Lady Mary was the sole surviving child of the Duke of Richmond and Lennox and heiress to his extensive property in Scotland. Besides this, she was, through her mother, a grand-daughter of the first Duke of Buckingham; and her son, if she had one, might well inherit the Buckingham property, for her uncle, the second duke, was childless. Six months after this marriage, on 29 April, the Countess of Ossory, then in Dublin with her husband, gave birth to a son, who was christened James after his grandfather. He was her second son; but the first, also James, had died within a few days of his birth. The Dublin-born James was to survive for just short of eighty years.

It was well for the duke and duchess, made happy by these events, that they could not see into the future. Within three years of her marriage the Countess of Arran was to die, childless, aged only eighteen. Ossory's son and heir, later the second Duke of Ormond, was to spend the last thirty years of his long life in exile; and with him the Ormond dukedom was to come to a sad, though not ignoble, end.

In the early 1660s these misfortunes were still in the future; but even at that time the Ormond family was not without its troubles. Elizabeth Butler's marriage to Lord Chesterfield, with which her mother had been so well satisfied, proved an unhappy one. There were, probably, faults on both sides. Chesterfield neglected his wife. She, young and thoughtless, enjoyed to the full the gay life of the court, where her beauty was much admired. This was a dangerous situation; and when the Duke of York, a notorious libertine, openly showed himself 'smitten in love with my Lady Chesterfield', as Pepys puts it, her husband was naturally alarmed. But he seems to

91

have regarded his wife, rather than the Duke, as the guilty party; and he banished her to Bretby Hall, the family seat in Derbyshire. This was in January 1663, while Ormond was still in Dublin, and he was at a loss what to do. He thought Chesterfield's conduct 'extravagant'; but he did not consider it wise that his daughter should, as she wished, come to her parents in Ireland, fearing that this might lead to a permanent separation. Some kind of reconciliation between husband and wife was patched up; but when the Ormonds came to England in the following year Lady Chesterfield was still in Derbyshire, where, as her letters show, she was very unhappy; and there she remained until her early death in July 1665. Her only child - Elizabeth, but more commonly called Betty - proved a continuing link between the two families; and Ormond, in his last years, was much concerned about finding a suitable husband for her.

While Lady Chesterfield lay dying in Derbyshire Ormond was with his wife at Moor Park, hoping, as he wrote to Arlington, that her 'tenderness and passion for her daughter... might receive some abatement by my presence'. But even in these circumstances his duty to the king came first. His letter was written at ten o'clock on a Monday evening and on Wednesday morning he was in attendance on the king.

The revision of the explanatory bill was now almost complete; and early in August it was ready to be read over to the king in council. Once that had been done Ormond could at last set off on his return journey. At this time London was in the grip of the plague and the court had moved to Salisbury. It was here that Ormond received, on 14 August, formal permission to pass into Ireland from any part of England, with his servants, his goods and one hundred horses, free from customs search or hindrance of any kind.

Starting as he did from Salisbury, his most convenient route was through South Wales to Milford Haven, from which the sea passage to Ireland was comparatively short. This route had the additional advantage of taking him into Somerset, of which he was lord lieutenant; and he used the opportunity to enquire into the state of the county and especially the militia. In Bristol he found the city so deeply divided by factions that the militia was in a wretched condition: 'greater desertions and worse soldiers in appearance and order I never saw anywhere'. He reported this state of affairs to Arlington, with some suggestions for improving it, and then continued his journey to

Gloucester and so, across the Severn, into Hereford. On Saturday, 2 September, almost three weeks after his departure from Salisbury, he and his retinue reached Milford Haven.

Here his secretary, Sir George Lane, was awaiting them with three frigates. The *Dartmouth* was reserved for the duke and duchess and Lady Arran, whose husband had already returned to Ireland, together with their personal attendants. The nobles and gentlemen who accompanied the duke were to sail in the *Pearl*. The *George* was to carry the horses. Shortly after five o'clock in the afternoon Lane added a hasty postscript to a letter he had written to Arlington: 'My lord and lady are just now come on board and we are hoisting sail with a fair gale'. Next day Ossory and Arran met them at sea; and about noon the whole party landed safely at Duncannon in Waterford Harbour.

After a brief stay in Waterford Ormond went to Kilkenny, where he remained for several weeks, since there was no point in summoning parliament until the bill of explanation had been printed and until a number of other bills that had been approved by the king and council in England had arrived. It was not until 17 October that he entered Dublin, where he was again given a splendid reception. On the 26th parliament re-assembled; and debates on the bill of explanation continued until the middle of December. But, as we have already seen, Ormond's influence prevailed; the measure passed safely through both houses; and, at least as far as that business was concerned, he could enjoy his Christmas with an easy mind.

(6)

The act of explanation did not put an end to the conflict over landed property. The dispossessed proprietors still had hopes of recovering what they had lost; and their claims were to be revived in the reign of James II. But though this issue fell for a time into the background, Ormond had other problems to contend with. Nothing had impressed him so much on his return to Ireland as the poverty of the country, an impression no doubt strengthened by the sharp contrast with the prosperity of England. Writing to Arlington from Kilkenny, a fortnight after his arrival, he drew a gloomy picture of the state of affairs:

> That which looks most threateningly upon us is the poverty
> of this people, a poverty so great and so apparent that in

93

good earnest I do not see how it will be possible for them to
pay what the parliament will charge them with for the
supply of the defect of the king's revenue.

Ormond attributed this poverty to acts of the English parliament 'that
obstruct, or rather, destroy our trade'; and though he expressed himself
in general terms it is probable that he had in mind an act of 1663
prohibiting the importation into England of Irish cattle between July
and December, the period when the trade was most profitable. Even
if, as is likely, he exaggerated the ill effect of this prohibition, there
could be no doubt that the Irish economy was dangerously weak.
Ormond himself realized this and he had already made an effort to
improve it by encouraging the woollen manufacture. Now, following
Strafford's example, he turned his attention to linen. Under his
direction skilled workers were brought over from France and from
the Netherlands; spinning-wheels were imported; prizes were offered
to encourage flax-cultivation and weaving; and protective duties were
imposed on imported linen goods.

These efforts to strengthen the economy could bring, at best, only
a slow improvement; and throughout the 1660s Ormond found, as he
had feared, that the revenue fell short of what was needed. As a
result, the pay of the army, by far the largest item of government
expenditure, was constantly in arrears. The danger inherent in this
situation was made clear by a mutiny among the four companies of
foot stationed at Carrickfergus. They had received no pay for a year;
and they were - at least according to their own account - on the verge
of starvation. In May 1666, when a revenue officer arrived in the
town with a large sum of money, they demanded that they should be
paid a part at least of what was due to them; and when this was
refused they mutinied and took possession of both the town and the
castle. News of this soon reached Dublin and Ormond at once sent
Arran, with four companies of guards, to Carrickfergus by sea; and he
himself hurried northwards with ten troops of horse. By the time he
arrived, however, Arran had suppressed the mutiny, and nothing
remained but to punish the mutineers. One hundred and ten of them
were tried by court martial and found guilty. Of these, nine were
hanged and the remainder were sentenced to be transported to the
plantations.

The severity of these sentences probably reflected Ormond's
conviction that there was more behind the mutiny than appeared and
that it was linked with a widespread conspiracy affecting not only the

province of Ulster but also south-western Scotland, where the government's ecclesiastical policy had aroused much unrest. In this he was almost certainly wrong; and he himself may have come to realize this, for the sentence of transportation was not carried out, and the men concerned were allowed, if they wished, to re-enlist in other companies.

Ormond did not remain long in the north. The Carrickfergus mutiny had interrupted a negotiation in which he was engaged with the Roman Catholic clergy, and by the first week in June he was back in Dublin. This negotiation had been initiated by Peter Walsh, a Franciscan friar who had supported Ormond against Rinuccini during the peace negotiations with the Confederates. His aim was to secure for the Roman Catholics a substantial measure of toleration in return for a declaration of their loyalty to the crown and a denial of papal authority in temporal matters. He had himself drawn up such a declaration - commonly called the 'Loyal Remonstrance' - and Ormond had sanctioned the meeting of a clerical congregation in Dublin to consider its terms. But the project came to nothing. Though Walsh proposed no more than the French clergy accepted some years later, he found very little support outside his own order; and the Remonstrance, as re-drafted by the clerical congregation, did not satisfy Ormond. He was free from the horror of 'popery' that was characteristic of protestantism at the time; but his experience during the 1640s had made him suspicious of clerical influence in politics, which the Remonstrance, in its original form, might (or so he hoped) have served to restrict. It was typical of the period that his conduct in this affair was attacked from both sides: by protestants, because he had allowed the clerical congregation to meet; by Roman Catholics because he had rejected the Remonstrance in its revised form. And it was typical of Ormond himself that he regarded both these attacks with equal indifference.

(7)

While Ormond was struggling with the problem of Irish government his position was being threatened by the course of politics in England. The influence of Clarendon's enemies was growing, both at court and in the country; and those who were working to secure his dismissal from the chancellorship were, with few exceptions, equally determined to have Ormond removed from the viceroyalty of Ireland. Among them all, the most active and most violent was the Duke of Buckingham, who seems to have regarded Ormond with a deep and lasting hatred for which it is difficult to find any reasonable ground. He took a leading part in passing through the English parliament a second and more stringent cattle act, which prohibited completely the importation of cattle from Ireland into England; and the terms in which he and his supporters urged the passage of the measure seemed almost to imply that it was directed against Ormond in person. Ossory, indeed, was so angered by Buckingham's language that he challenged him to a duel, which the duke managed to avoid, though not without arousing some doubts about his courage.

The passage of this measure showed clearly that parliament was now dominated by the faction opposed to Clarendon and Ormond; and it was doubtful how long the king, who depended upon parliament for money, could continue to retain them in office. Reluctant, as always, to face any unpleasant decision, he delayed month after month; and it was not until the end of August 1667 that he dismissed Clarendon from the chancellorship. He was not yet, however, prepared to part with Ormond also; and after the dismissal of Clarendon he wrote to reassure him:

> I have not in the least diminished the value and kindness I ever had for you, which I thought fit to say upon this occasion, because it is very possible malicious people may suggest the contrary to you.

Clarendon himself had already written to Ormond; and his account of the position comes nearer the truth:

> God prosper you and yours, and keep your master true to you; for I believe I have few enemies who do not desire to oblige you the way they have done me.

Clarendon's warning was well founded. When the English parliament re-assembled in February 1668 an attempt, instigated by Buckingham, was made to frame charges against Ormond that would justify his impeachment. The attempt came to nothing, for none of the charges brought forward could survive investigation; but Ormond's enemies still hoped to bring him into discredit with the king and used all their influence to that end. Ossory, who was in London and kept a watchful eye on his father's interests, was anxious about the situation. Some months earlier he had suggested, in a letter to his mother, that Ormond should ask the king for permission to go to London, while

Ossory himself went to Ireland as lord deputy. Ormond had at first been reluctant to follow this course; but the threat of an impeachment, though in the end it came to nothing, seems to have changed his mind. In mid-December he wrote to the king as Ossory had advised and received the permission for which he had asked. It was not, however, until March that Ossory arrived in Dublin; but once he was there Ormond was free, if he chose, to go to London to defend his position.

It may seem at first sight strange that Ormond was now so anxious to retain the viceroyalty, which he had accepted reluctantly and only because it was the king's wish that he should do so. It was, however, natural that he should be unwilling to lay down the office in circumstances that would inevitably give colour to the charges of misgovernment that his enemies had brought against him. Besides this, he was concerned about his financial position. The king had assigned him large sums to discharge the debts he had incurred in the royal service; and the Irish parliament had voted him a grant of £30,000. But so far he had received only part of what was due to him; if he were now removed from office the remainder might never be paid; and the likelihood of his being able to free himself from debt would be greatly reduced.

Though Ormond was anxious to defend his position, he was not easily convinced that a journey to London was necessary; and for some weeks after Ossory's arrival in Dublin he still hesitated. What decided him to go was the news that Roger Boyle, Earl of Orrery and president of Munster, was planning a visit to court. Boyle was one of the most astute politicians of the period. He had changed sides more than once during the 1640s and 1650s; he had held an influential office during the protectorate, but had been one of the first to come out openly in favour of the restoration of monarchy and had been rewarded with an earldom and the presidency of Munster. He was not a man whose professions of friendship were to be trusted; and Ormond suspected that his proposed visit to court at this time was intended to forward his own interests, and most probably at Ormond's expense. In these circumstances Ormond decided that if Orrery was to be at court then he had better be there too. On Friday, 24 April, he set sail from Dublin; next day he landed at Holyhead; and on 6 May he reached London, some weeks ahead of Orrery, whose journey had been delayed by an attack of gout.

Since Ormond's enemies depended mainly upon Orrery for the evidence necessary to support the charges they meant to bring against his administration, the opening of their attack had to be delayed. During the interval Ormond's confidence grew stronger. On 19 May he wrote to Ossory:

> The king seems well satisfied with the account I gave him of the management of his affairs, and not at all disposed to take them out of my hands.

By a curious coincidence an entry of the same date in Samuel Pepys's diary provides evidence of the king's regard for Ormond's opinion: 'Since my lord of Ormond's coming over', he had been told by an acquaintance, 'the king begins to be mightily reclaimed, and sups every night with great pleasure with the queen'.

Ormond's influence on the king's domestic life, whether or not so great as Pepys implies, was certainly not lasting; and his influence in other respects was threatened by the arrival of Orrery in June. Orrery undertook to show that the revenue of Ireland was more than sufficient to meet all the charges of the civil and military establishments and that the large debt accumulated during Ormond's administration must therefore be the result of mismanagement. The subsequent investigation of Irish finances dragged on during many weeks; and, though it did not provide evidence of maladministration on Ormond's part, it gave his enemies an opportunity to cast doubts upon his efficiency and to suggest to the king that a change in the government of Ireland was likely to improve the situation.

During this critical period in Ormond's fortunes his reaction to the course of events can be traced in his letters to Ossory. At the end of June he reported that he was assured of the support of Arlington, whose marriage to Isabella van Beverweert had made him Ossory's brother-in-law. But Arlington's support was little more than passive, for he was unwilling to risk a quarrel with Buckingham, Ormond's most powerful enemy. By September, Ormond had become convinced that he was losing ground and that the king might already have decided that he should not return to Ireland as lord lieutenant. But he was determined not to give way voluntarily: 'I resolve not to part with the government by any offer of my own'; and he thought that his enemies might find it difficult to persuade the king to dismiss him. In this he was certainly right; and they were obliged to propose a compromise: he was to remain in England; and the government of Ireland was to be in the hands of two or three lord justices, of whom Ossory would be one. For several weeks he was under strong pressure, especially from Arlington, to accept this compromise. In a letter of

21 November to Ossory he describes at some length the argument put forward by Arlington and others; but he concludes with the good news that the king was on his side:

> I come just now from a long discourse with the king, and from receiving all the satisfaction I can wish, and the assurance I can desire, that no suggestions to my prejudice have or will have place or credit with him. And at my going forth, he commanded me to rest confident of his justice and favour to me.

Ormond seems to have been convinced by this re-assurance; and, as time passed, his confidence grew stronger. In a letter to Ossory of 9 February 1669 he declared his firm belief that 'the king neither is, nor will be, prevailed upon to remove me from the government of Ireland, or to make any alteration in it'. But the event was soon to show that his judgement was at fault. He had assumed that Charles's expressions of friendship were to be taken at their face value; and he underestimated the influence of Buckingham and his allies. Within a few days he was to be undeceived. On 14 February, in the committee of foreign affairs (which was, in fact, a kind of cabinet) the king announced his intention of removing Ormond from the lord lieutenancy, paying tribute to his long and faithful service, and named Lord Robartes, the lord privy seal, as his successor.

CHAPTER VIII

Out of Favour

(1)

The period between Ormond's removal from the viceroyalty in 1669 and his re-appointment in 1677 formed an interlude in his long career. From early manhood until beyond his seventy-fifth birthday he was, apart from these years, continuously engaged in the royal service at home or abroad, and always in posts where much depended upon his ability, his courage and his unselfish devotion to the crown. What gives this period its special character, however, is not so much that Ormond was out of office as that he was out of favour.

When the king announced his decision to remove him from the viceroyalty he had declared - so Ormond reported to Ossory - 'how well he was satisfied with my thirty years service to his father and himself; that the change he now made was not out of distrust or displeasure, as should appear by admitting me into the most secret and important parts of his affairs, and that nobody should have a higher place in his esteem and confidence'. A complimentary speech made on such an occasion is not to be taken at its face value; and Charles, who was already more than half committed to the policy that led in the following year to the treaty of Dover, had very good reasons for not admitting Ormond into 'the most secret and important parts of his affairs'. It is not so easy, however, to understand the ostentatious neglect with which he now treated him. When Ormond appeared at court, which he did almost daily, the king rarely recognized his presence and even more rarely spoke to him; and all who enjoyed, or hoped to enjoy, the royal favour naturally followed his example.

Ormond found this treatment hard to endure, as he admitted in a letter written a few years later; but he did not allow any sign of resentment to appear, maintaining a calm and cheerful demeanour, never complaining of the king's neglect, or even appearing to notice it. No doubt he was influenced by his strong sense of loyalty and believed that it was his duty to submit without complaint to the treatment he received from the king; but he also knew that any sign of discontent on his part would add to the triumph of his enemies. Day after day he appeared at court bearing the white staff that was the symbol of his office as lord steward of the household, a position that the king had allowed him to keep, since it carried no political influence. If people were willing to talk to him, as occasionally happened, he conversed cheerfully; if he were left to himself he appeared equally well satisfied. On one occasion his calm assurance so impressed Buckingham, who would risk anything for a jest, that he asked the king 'whether it be the Duke of Ormond that is out of favour with Your Majesty, or Your Majesty that is out of favour with the Duke of Ormond, for of the two you really look most out of countenance'. Buckingham's purpose was no doubt to embarrass the king; but in so doing he paid, however unintentionally, a tribute to Ormond.

It might have seemed natural that Ormond, out of office and out of favour, should retire to Ireland; and this had at one time been his intention. Some months earlier, while his future was still in doubt, he had written to Ossory: '...if I were to-morrow out of the government I would if I could go to Ireland'. But when the time came he was obliged to remain in London: partly because he was engaged in negotiations for the payment of money still due to him from the crown; partly because his enemies, not satisfied with having secured his removal from office, were trying to make out charges that would justify his impeachment. But even after the attempt at impeachment had been abandoned and he had done what he could to set his finances in order, he remained in England for almost four years longer. One reason for this delay was a change in the viceroyalty. His successor, Lord Robartes, had been recalled, at his own request, barely six months after his arrival in Dublin; and his successor, Lord Berkeley of Stratton, was a man under whose government Ormond was unwilling to live. Not only was his administration notoriously corrupt, but he was closely allied with Ormond's bitter enemy, Richard Talbot and his brother, Peter Talbot, the titular archbishop of Dublin. But even after Berkeley had been replaced, in May 1672, by Arthur Capel, Earl of Essex, for whom Ormond had a high regard, he still remained in England for two years longer. It seems not unlikely that his reluctance to leave London was due, in part at least, to a lingering hope that he might, by some means, be restored to the king's favour.

(2)

Ormond's removal from the viceroyalty had meant a substantial reduction in his income, and this at a time when he was striving to reduce his burden of debt, much of it incurred in the king's service. It was to this end that in the summer of 1670 he sold Moor Park to the Duke of Monmouth for £11,000, no small sacrifice for a man so fond as Ormond was of country life and country sports. Almost at the same time the duchess noted with satisfaction that they were about to save £250 a year in rent: Lord Cornbury had lent them a part of Clarendon House, the huge house built by his father, the former chancellor. But six months later she had forgotten about the saving in rent and was much concerned about the cost of the lavish hospitality that the duke's position obliged them to provide. 'We are forced', she writes, 'into the expense of our keeping a great table not possible to be avoided, having daily the resort of all strangers and ambassadors, and all the nobility besides'.

The duchess's complaint about the expense involved in entertaining a constant succession of distinguished guests is a clear indication that Ormond, though out of favour at court, was still an important figure in public life. But there is other and more telling evidence to the same effect. In August 1669, within a few months of his removal from the viceroyalty, he was elected chancellor of the university of Oxford, an office in which he succeeded Archbishop Sheldon of Canterbury, on whose recommendation he was chosen. Later in the same year a group of M.P.s - who called themselves 'the church and cavalier party' - included in their programme a resolution 'to adhere to the Duke of Ormond against all opposition'. Ormond himself kept aloof from party politics; but all who combined devotion to the Church of England with loyalty to the crown regarded him as one of their champions.

It was shortly after he had moved to Clarendon House that Ormond experienced the most dangerous adventure of his life. On 6 December 1670 he was among the guests at a banquet given by the Lord Mayor of London in honour of Prince William of Orange (afterwards King William III), who was then on a visit to England. Though in those days people dined much earlier than now, the function lasted so long that it was dark by the time Ormond entered his coach to return to Clarendon House, which lay on the outskirts of the city, about a

103

quarter of a mile to the north of St. James's Palace. As the coach made its way slowly up St. James's Street a group of armed men stopped it and one of them dragged Ormond out, threw him across a horse and rode off.

Ormond's footmen, who should have been in close attendance, three on each side of the coach, had lingered behind; and there was no effective resistance to the sudden attack. But the alarm was soon given and the pursuit began. Ormond, though now sixty years of age, was still strong and active; he managed to unseat his captor; both fell to the ground; and while they struggled there the rescue party arrived. The attackers, having fired a few shots at random, made off; and Ormond, shaken and bruised, but not seriously injured, was carried home.

The leader of this attack was Thomas Blood, who had been at the head of the conspiracy to seize Dublin Castle in 1663. But this was not known at the time; and it might never have come to light had not Blood, only a few months later, engaged in another, and even more daring, enterprise - the theft of the crown and other regalia from the Tower of London. In this he was detected, when almost on the point of success; and though the evidence against him was irrefutable, he managed, by some mysterious means, to obtain an interview with the king. In the course of this interview he confessed that it was he who had planned and led the attack upon Ormond and that he had intended to carry him off to Tyburn and hang him there, in revenge for the execution of four of his fellow-conspirators in the Castle plot. The outcome of this strange interview was that the king granted him a pardon for his attempt to steal the crown and also promised to pardon him for the attack upon Ormond, provided that Ormond himself would agree. All this was mysterious enough. Even more mysterious was the fact that Blood now received from the king an estate worth £500 a year and became a regular frequenter of the court: about a year later John Evelyn met him as a guest at a dinner in the house of Sir Thomas Clifford, treasurer of the household and one of the king's most trusted advisers.

This strangely generous treatment of a self-confessed thief and would-be assassin was attributed by many contemporaries to the influence of Buckingham. Ossory went further and declared that it was Buckingham who had himself inspired the attempt on his father's life. As a precaution against any repetition of such an attempt he warned Buckingham, in the king's presence, that if Ormond came to a violent end by sword, pistol or poison, he would know that Buckingham was responsible; and, he concluded, 'wherever I meet you I shall pistol you, though you stood behind the king's chair; and I tell it you in his majesty's presence, that you may be sure I shall keep my word'. Though this story comes to us at third hand, it is so characteristic of Ossory's impulsive nature and of his devotion to his father that there is little reason to doubt its essential truth.[1] Ormond himself took the attempted assassination and its aftermath much more calmly than his son. When asked for his consent to the pardoning of Blood he replied at once that he could easily forgive him for attempting to take his life since the king had forgiven him for attempting to steal his crown.

(3)

Ossory's outspoken support of his father did not prevent his advancement in the royal service; and Ormond, throughout the period of his own exclusion from favour, could still take pride in the distinguished career of his eldest and favourite son. In the early stages of the Restoration period Ossory's standing at court had depended largely on the patronage of the Duke of York; but within a short time he had risen so high in the favour of the king himself that he did not need to depend on any other influence to ensure his advancement, In 1662 he was made an earl in the peerage of Ireland.[2] In 1666 he was made an English baron as Lord Butler of Moore Park; and in the same year he was appointed a gentleman of the king's bedchamber and a member of the English privy council. In 1670 and 1671 he commanded the fleet of yachts that escorted the Prince of Orange on his visit to England and on his return to Holland. But Ossory's popular reputation, of which his father was naturally proud, depended less on these official functions than on his exploits in war. In the 'Four Days' Battle' between the English and Dutch fleets, in June 1666, he served as a volunteer on board Albemarle's flagship,

1. The story first appeared in print in the second volume of Thomas Carte's biography of Ormond (1736). Carte heard the story from Robert Lesley of Glasslough, who had it from Francis Turner, one of the royal chaplains (afterwards bishop of Ely), who was present on the occasion.
2. From 1643, when Ormond was made a marquess, his eldest son was, by courtesy, styled Earl of Ossory; but he remained, in law, a commoner - in 1661 he was elected to the Irish house of commons as one of the members for the University of Dublin, of which his father was Chancellor.

the *Royal Charles*; and he so distinguished himself that he became, according to contemporary accounts, 'the darling of the English nation'. When war with the Dutch broke out again in March 1672 he was appointed to the command of a ship; and by the time the war ended, in February 1674, he had risen to the rank of admiral.

During the interval between the two wars the king had shown how high Ossory stood in his favour by appointing him a Knight of the Garter in September 1672; and in the following month he was installed at Windsor. Ormond himself had been a member of the order since 1649 - a period when the ceremony of installation had perforce been omitted - and both he and the duchess were present on this occasion. The ceremony necessarily involved Ossory in considerable expense, towards which Ormond contributed £500. The duchess, who often preached the need for economy, though she rarely practised it, was somewhat uneasy about this outlay; but she herself presented Ossory with a diamond George, though she seems to have found some difficulty in raising the £200 that it cost her.

Ormond's other sons were, at this time, a source of anxiety rather than of comfort to their parents. Arran, overcome with grief at his wife's death in July 1668, had begun to drink heavily; and more than two years later the duchess was still disturbed by the reports she heard of 'his strange way of life'. But Arran, though he remained fond of good drink and jovial company, recovered his self-control. In 1672 he went to sea with the Duke of York and took part in the battle of Southwold Bay, along with his elder brother, who was then in command of the *Victory*. In June of the following year he married Dorothy, daughter of John Ferrars of Tamworth Castle, in Warwickshire. Two months later he was again at sea; and he so distinguished himself at the battle of the Texel that he was made an English peer. Later on, after Ossory's death in July 1680, he was to become his father's most faithful and most useful supporter.

The third son, Lord John, is said to have been 'very agreeable in his person and conversation'; but contemporary correspondence reveals him as a man fond of drink and low company and constantly in debt. His parents had no illusions about his character. When a County Dublin gentleman who was restoring a church on his estate told Ormond that Lord John had presented a board with a table of the ten commandments, to be placed (as was then customary) behind the altar, Ormond replied drily that it was easy for a man to give away what he had no desire to keep. The duchess was even more outspoken: she described Lord John as 'so little regarded in the world that nobody does or can commend him for any one good quality'.

It may have been in the hope that marriage would improve Lord John's character that his parents arranged a match between him and Lady Ann Chichester, only daughter of the Earl of Donegall; and the king, despite the fact that Ormond was still out of favour, marked the occasion by raising Lord John to the peerage as Earl of Gowran. The marriage took place in January 1675; but if it did anything to reform John's way of life the change came too late. His health had been hopelessly undermined; and eighteen months later he died in Paris, where he had gone in the hope of finding effective medical treatment. His widow married Francis Aungier, afterwards Earl of Longford; but the connection with the Ormonds still survived. The duchess spoke of Lady Longford as 'my daughter Longford'; and the earl was one of Ormond's most faithful friends during the troubled period of the Popish Plot.

Before the negotiations for Lord John's marriage had begun the first marriage in the next generation of the family had taken place. In July 1673 Ossory's eldest daughter, Elizabeth, had married William George Richard Stanley, ninth Earl of Derby. The bride was only thirteen and the bridegroom barely three years older; and for some years after the marriage Elizabeth, now Countess of Derby, continued to live with her parents. The earl, whose guardianship Ormond had undertaken, was sent abroad with a tutor to complete his education. He proved a very troublesome charge: in Paris he quickly got into bad company, defied his tutor's authority and finally dismissed him. Ormond, to whom both appealed, acted promptly. In place of the tutor, who was glad to be relieved of his troublesome task, he appointed Colonel Thomas Fairfax, a younger son of the first Lord Fairfax, who told Derby firmly that he had been sent to govern him and that he would govern him. In this he succeeded; and some time later, while he and his pupil were travelling in Italy, he was able to report that 'my Lord of Derby left Rome with as good a reputation as any of his quality that have been here'. Derby himself sent a long account of his meeting with an English physician resident in Rome, James Alban Gibbes, on whom the university of Oxford had, at Ormond's request, conferred the degree of M.D., despite the fact that he was a Roman

Catholic.[1] Derby's later career was undistinguished; and Ossory thought him a selfish husband. But, in one respect at least, his conduct was such as Ormond could heartily approve: he was among those who, in King James's reign, gave up office rather than act contrary to the interests of the Church of England.

(4)

While the negotiations for his third son's marriage were still in progress Ormond had returned to Ireland. By the early summer of 1673 he had grown weary of his long neglect at court and had almost made up his mind to retire to Kilkenny. But while the war with the Dutch was in progress and while royal policy was under attack in parliament he felt it his duty to remain and support the king in the house of lords - not, perhaps, without some hope of recovering his former influence. A year later the country was at peace; but though his arch-enemy, Buckingham, was out of office and in disgrace with the king, Ormond found himself as much out of favour as before. In June 1674 he wrote to the king, asking for permission to go to Ireland. His letter, though perfectly respectful in its language, barely conceals his sense of grievance at the treatment he had received:

> It is now six years since I came over last; and a great part of that time I have passed more uneasily than I made show of, or than I ever thought I should do in your majesty's court and presence, having had many reasons to believe your favour was at least very much abated towards me. The circumstances were too many and too little pleasing to me, to reckon them up; but they were such as seemed to evidence to the world, that it was rather the remembrance of some old service I had endeavoured to do the crown, than anything else that preserved me from the utmost disgrace due to a faulty and insignificant person. How grievous soever this was to me, I have borne it with duty, and more temper than I am naturally master of.

The king granted the permission asked for; and very shortly afterwards the duke and duchess left London. They spent a fortnight at Bath, in the hope that the waters might stave off the attack of gout from which Ormond now suffered every winter, and then moved on

1. Gibbes is now remembered, in so far as he is remembered at all, for his Latin verse rather than for his medical skill.

to Minehead, where they took ship on 27 June. Next day they landed at Waterford and were soon at home in Kilkenny Castle. Here they had ample evidence that though the duke might be out of favour at court his standing in Ireland was as high as ever. So great were the numbers of the nobility and gentry who came to greet him and the duchess on their return that during the next couple of weeks there was hardly a day when fewer than two hundred guests were entertained in the castle. But at the end of that period Ormond felt that he could delay no longer in paying his respects to the lord lieutenant, the Earl of Essex; and he set off for Dublin.

Essex received him somewhat coldly. His own position at this time was far from secure; and he may well have feared that any cordiality shown to Ormond would be reported in London and turned to his disadvantage. Ormond himself probably understood the reason for Essex's lack of cordiality, and he refused to take offence - he flatly denied having said, as was reported both in Dublin and in London, that the lord lieutenant had received him 'according to his breeding and understanding'. But he did cut short his visit to Dublin and retired to Kilkenny, where he could enjoy the country life that he loved. Not long after his return he received from Lord Aungier the welcome present of two casts of hawks, with the promise of a visit in a few weeks' time, when their qualities would be put to the test.

After his return from Dublin Ormond remained in Kilkenny until the spring of 1675; and he would probably have remained longer but that he felt it his duty to be in London for the meeting of parliament, which was due to take place in April. He had some difficulty in arranging transport, for his agent in Dublin could find no ship large enough to convey the duke and duchess, their retinue of attendants, their coach-horses and the great mass of luggage that such a company required. In these circumstances Ormond made use of his position as one of the commissioners of the admiralty and wrote to Ossory suggesting that the navy might provide a ship to transport them. But it was the king himself who settled the matter. Fearing that parliament, when it met, might prove troublesome he was anxious that Ormond, on whose support he knew he could depend, should be present; and he sent a frigate, the *Norwich*, to Waterford to take him and his party on board. Before parliament met, on 13 April, Ormond was in London. As things turned out his support was not needed. Buckingham and Shaftesbury, now united in opposition to the king, were outvoted in the house of lords. It was in the commons that the opposition proved most dangerous; and on 9 June the king prorogued parliament to October.

Ormond had intended to return to Ireland after the prorogation of parliament and he had received the king's permission to do so. But he was obliged to remain in London to defend himself against charges of financial mismanagement during his viceroyalty in the 1660s, brought against him by Richard Jones, Viscount Ranelagh. In August 1671 Ranelagh and a number of others had entered into an agreement with the crown - generally referred to as 'Ranelagh's undertaking' - by which they were to receive the whole revenue of Ireland and to become responsible for meeting all the charges of the civil and military establishments. According to Ranelagh's calculations there would be a substantial surplus; and this was to reward him and his partners for their labours. When the period during which the undertaking was to last ended in the summer of 1675 it was found that payments due in almost all departments of government were heavily in arrears; and Ranelagh's accounts were in a state of utter confusion. He defended himself on the ground that the fault lay with Ormond, who, he declared, had left the administration heavily in debt and the finances in hopeless disorder. Ormond was determined to defend himself; and he received from the king a promise that the matter would be thoroughly investigated; and it was not until May 1676 that the king declared himself fully satisfied that there had been no mismanagement of the finances during Ormond's viceroyalty and ordered an entry to this effect to be made in the minutes of the council.

Even after this business had been settled Ormond remained in England; and he did not return to Ireland until a year later, when he went as lord lieutenant. Thomas Carte, whose massive biography is still, after more than two and a half centuries, the standard authority for Ormond's career, passes over this period very quickly and writes as if his re-appointment to the viceroyalty came as a surprise to Ormond himself. The truth is, however, that since the summer of 1675 Essex's friends in England had been warning him that he might be recalled; and, though not until some months later, they commonly mentioned Ormond as a possible successor. These reports no doubt reflected opinions current at court; but they would not have been so consistent and circumstantial had there not been good reason to believe that the king intended to make a change in the government of Ireland. It was the hope that this change would mean his own re-appointment as lord lieutenant that kept Ormond in London; and when this hope was fulfilled he was probably more surprised by the manner in which the king announced his appointment than by the appointment itself. One day in April 1677 the king, who had taken little notice of Ormond since his return to court two years earlier, sent a message announcing that he would sup with him that evening. The duchess made sure that the entertainment was worthy of the guest; and before he departed Charles let Ormond know that he was to succeed Essex as Lord lieutenant of Ireland. On the following day, when Ormond appeared at court, the king made the appointment public:

> Yonder comes Ormond; I have done all I can to disoblige that man, and make him as discontented as others, but he will not be out of humour with me, he will be loyal in spite of my teeth. I must even take him in again, and he is the fittest man to govern Ireland.

Ormond was anxious that Essex, for whom he had a genuine regard, should not believe that he had been intriguing against him. On 20 April, a few days after the king's announcement of the coming change, he wrote to Essex assuring him that this was not so. A week later Essex replied, fully accepting Ormond's professions of friendship and promising to keep him informed of all important business during the interval that must elapse before the change of government took place.

On the same day as that on which he wrote to Essex Ormond wrote also to George Mathew,[1] with instructions about the preparations to be made for his arrival in Dublin. But many weeks passed before he was ready to set out. His commission as lord lieutenant was not sealed until 24 May; after that the framing of his formal instructions took a good deal of time; and it was not until the beginning of August that he began his journey to Chester. As was usual when he travelled as lord lieutenant, he was accompanied by a train of coaches and moved by easy stages. At Oxford, which he had not visited since his installation as chancellor eight years earlier, he remained for two nights; and among the nobles and gentlemen who were created doctors on this occasion was his second son, Richard, Earl of Arran. It was not until almost three weeks after he had set out that he reached

1. See above; page 8, note 1.

111

Dublin, where Essex had prepared a splendid reception; and on Thursday, 24 May he received from his predecessor the sword of state, the symbol of office, and was sworn in, for the third time, as lord lieutenant of Ireland.

CHAPTER IX

The Popish Plot

(1)

When Ormond became lord lieutenant of Ireland for the third time he was approaching the end of his sixty-seventh year, which was a much more advanced age in the seventeenth century than it would be considered today. Among the leading political figures of the Restoration period few lived so long. Albemarle, for example, died at sixty-one, Clarendon at sixty-five, Lauderdale at sixty-six; of the five members of the Cabal, Arlington, who lived longest, died at sixty-eight. But Ormond, despite his age, was still in good health; and, as he assured Ossory in the spring of 1678, almost as active as ever, though he admitted in the same sentence that he could not expect to remain so for more than a few years longer. It is easy, then, to understand why he should have wished to be restored to the king's favour and take some share in the direction of affairs. But why should he have been eager, as he undoubtedly was, to spend his last years of active life in the arduous task of governing Ireland?

A part, at least, of the answer appears clearly enough in his correspondence: he hoped that the income of the office would enable him to pay off his debts and make better provision for his family. The duchess shared this hope; and hardly a month after their arrival in Dublin she wrote optimistically: 'I hope my lord's affairs are now so regulated as he will be able to pay off a considerable part of his debt, and yet support the dignity of his place in a way of honour and credit to him'. Ormond certainly made sure that he maintained the dignity of his place; but there is no evidence to suggest that he was able, as Essex had been, to lay aside each year £4,000 out of his emoluments. Quite apart from the cost of maintaining his own household with the splendour befitting a viceroy who was also at the head of the Irish nobility, both his surviving sons were still to some extent dependent upon him; and they too must live in a style befitting their rank and ancestry. The provision he made for the education of Ossory's heir, James, afterwards second Duke of Ormond, gives some idea of the standard he sought to maintain.

Early in 1679 James, then in his fourteenth year, was sent to Oxford. Ormond, as chancellor of the university, could naturally exercise a good deal of influence; and James was placed under the care of the bishop, John Fell,[1] who was also dean of Christchurch. The establishment provided for him consisted of a tutor (Peter Drelincourt, afterwards dean of Armagh),[2] a *valet de chambre*, two footmen, a groom and two or three horses. The cost, borne by Ormond, was reckoned to be £1,000 a year - more, that is, than the income of many a country gentleman. What we know of James's Oxford career does not suggest that it had much to do with making him what he was later considered to be - 'the best bred man of his age'.

The provision made for the education of his grandson gives a fair idea of the standard of living that Ormond felt obliged to maintain; and the income from his estates, extensive though they were, would have been barely sufficient for his needs, even if he had not been encumbered by a load of debt. But it would be unfair to conclude that his desire to resume the viceroyalty arose solely from the prospect of financial advantage. Almost the whole of his adult life had been spent in the service of the crown; and he could not easily reconcile himself to the idea of being laid aside while he still felt capable of being useful; and where could he be more useful than in Ireland? He does not, indeed, anywhere express himself openly in these terms; but it is an attitude that can easily be deduced from his correspondence. One thing is certain: whatever may be said about Ormond's reasons for desiring the viceroyalty, it was well both for Ireland and for the king that he was at the head of the Irish administration during the critical period that opened soon after his arrival in Dublin.

1. Fell is best remembered as the subject of a quatrain by Tom Brown, based on an epigram of Martial:
  I do not love thee Dr. Fell,
  The reason why I cannot tell;
  But this I know and know full well,
  I do not love thee Dr. Fell.
2. Drelincourt, though he acquired some reputation as an author in his own time, is now remembered only because Defoe's *Apparition of Mrs Veal* was appended to the fourth edition of his *Christian's defence against the fear of death*.

The most urgent task facing Ormond when he took up office was to set the finances in order. On paper, the revenue was more than sufficient to meet all the charges upon it; but there had been so much corruption in its management that the treasury was empty and the pay of the army heavily in arrears. As a first step towards setting things right Ormond proposed to summon a parliament, which would, he was confident, supply the funds needed to meet all outstanding debts. Charles, after some hesitation, gave his consent; and preparations for a meeting of parliament were set in train. This was a long-drawn-out business; and before the necessary preparations had been completed the whole situation, both in Ireland and in England, had been changed by Titus Oates's revelation, in September 1678, of an alleged 'Popish Plot'. For more than two years thereafter the maintenance of peace in Ireland, and perhaps even the fate of the monarchy, depended very much upon Ormond's refusal to be frightened or coerced into dangerously repressive measures.

At his first appearance before the English council Oates had little to say about Ireland, beyond asserting that the plotters intended to murder Ormond as well as the king. But the unscrupulous politicians - among whom Shaftesbury was the ablest and most ambitious - who hoped to use for their own ends the excitement stirred up by Oates's allegations,. were determined that Ireland must be involved. Their minds went back to 1641, when the Irish insurrection had helped to bring about the final break between Charles I and his opponents; and, in any case, a 'Popish Plot' in which Ireland, with its predominantly Roman Catholic population, was not involved, might soon lose credibility. Once it became known that stories of an Irish plot were readily accepted in England and that those who carried them were well rewarded scores of informers flocked across the channel; and their allegations, however extravagant, were believed by the public and used by the politicians.

Most of these informers were men whose word would, in normal circumstances, carry little weight. They are, wrote Ormond, 'such creatures as no schoolboy would trust them with the design for the robbing of an orchard'; and he sums up the value of their evidence in a brief but telling sentence: 'As they have not the honesty to swear truth so they have not the wit to invent probably'. But the panic-stricken English public was easily imposed upon; and the evidence of these informers was skilfully used by Shaftesbury and his allies to promote their own ends.

Not all tales of an Irish plot came from such witnesses as Ormond described. Orrery, who had now retired to his estates in Munster, sent him one letter after another about suspicious characters and suspicious happenings. Ormond replied to each in turn and made such investigations as he could; but not one of Orrery's reports proved true. He had, for example, made a great stir about a ship bound for Ireland, loaded with arms to equip a rebel army. The ship was identified and, when it reached port, searched: it proved to be loaded not with arms but - appropriately enough - salt. Ormond dealt patiently with his old rival who, he suggested in a letter to Sir Robert Southwell, busied himself about public affairs as a means of 'diverting the pain of his gout'. Ossory took a less charitable view: to him, Orrery was 'the charlatan of Munster'.

Though Ormond did not believe that there was any 'popish plot' in Ireland, he knew that the resentment caused by the acts of settlement and explanation was still strong; and he feared that any harsh measures might provoke a violent reaction. He was obliged to obey the instructions he received; but he acted as cautiously as he could. Thus, for example, when he was ordered to disarm all papists he issued a proclamation directing them to hand in their arms within twenty days. For this he was sharply criticized in England and told that he should have sent troops to search every Catholic house in the country. He made the very reasonable defence that if an insurrection was, as his critics alleged, being prepared it would be madness to scatter the army in small detachments here and there throughout the country. But he also had in mind another consideration, though he did not include it in his reports to London. He thought it not improbable that soldiers engaged in searching houses might behave in such a way as to arouse some violent reaction and that incidents of this sort, even if they did not lead to any open insurrection, would be used as evidence that Ireland was dangerously unsettled.

Ormond's cautious policy did not satisfy Shaftesbury and his allies. It would be unfair to say that they deliberately sought to provoke an insurrection in Ireland; but they were determined to prove that an insurrection had been planned and to claim the credit of having frustrated the attempt. Ormond was too honest to provide the evidence they wanted; and his wise caution in executing the instructions he received prevented the sporadic violence that would have served their purpose. They were determined, therefore, to have him replaced by a viceroy on whom they could rely; and they missed no opportunity of criticizing his conduct of affairs.

During this difficult period Ossory, who was then in London, was his father's constant ally and adviser. 'I think it my duty', he wrote, 'to inform you of every little thing, that, when you see the malice of your enemies, and in what they endeavour your prejudice, you may be the better able to defend yourself against them'. His position as a gentleman of the king's bedchamber gave him high standing at court; and he was not a man to let any criticism of his father that might be made there pass unchallenged. Besides this, his exploits at sea had made him a national hero; and this no doubt gave added weight to his words when he had an opportunity not only to defend Ormond but also to make a counter-attack against Shaftesbury. A newly-elected parliament met in March 1679; and Shaftesbury's supporters were so strong in both houses that he might hope to have Ormond replaced by a viceroy acceptable to himself. Early in the session he made a long and powerful speech on Irish affairs, suggesting very clearly that Ireland was not safe in Ormond's hands. Ossory at once rose to defend his father. He first disposed of Shaftesbury's charges, direct and indirect, against Ormond and then moved from defence to attack in a telling denunciation of Shaftesbury political record:

> Having spoke of what he [Ormond] has done, I presume with the same truth to tell your lordships what he has not done. He never advised the breaking of the triple league; he never advised the shutting up of the exchequer; he never advised the declaration for a toleration; he never advised the falling out with the Dutch and the joining with France; he was not the author of that most excellent position of *Delenda est Carthago*, that Holland, a protestant country, should, contrary to the true interests of England, be totally destroyed. I beg your lordships will be so just as to judge of my father, and of all men, according to their actions and counsels.

This speech made a considerable impression not only at home but in Holland, where it was translated into Dutch and printed.[1] It certainly had some effect upon Shaftesbury, for a few weeks later

1. Prince William, with whom Ossory had long been on friendly terms, wrote to congratulate him on his speech.

Ossory could report to his mother:

> My Lord Shaftesbury and I had a long discussion, wherein
> he assured me of his value for me, and respect for our
> family, upon which we parted upon fair terms, he assuring
> me he would first tell me his exceptions, if he had any, and
> I undertook to satisfy his doubts all I could.

In the hope that this understanding might be strengthened Ormond's
friends persuaded him to write to Shaftesbury. How reluctantly he
undertook the task appears from his own account in a letter to Sir
Robert Southwell:

> I have found some difficulty to write to my Lord Shaftesbury
> at all, and when I had overcome that with the help of the
> deference I have for the opinion of my friends, I found it
> harder to pen such a letter as could at once meet their sense
> and satisfy the great man and myself.

It proved lost labour. Within a short time Shaftesbury's agents were
again at work, spreading reports that Ormond was neglecting the
protestant interest in Ireland. Others were equally active: Essex, as
Ossory reported to his father, 'makes it his work to catch hold of
anything that may prejudice you'; and under such patronage the
rumour-mongers naturally flourished. In April 1680, for example, it
was the gossip of the London coffee-houses that Ormond and Ossory
were planning to betray Ireland to the French.

Ossory took such accusations lightly and assured his father that
'the visible falsity of those reports have rather done us good than
harm'. At least so far as he himself was concerned, this was probably
true, for he seems to have been universally popular, even with those
who did not share his views. Three months later, when he lay dying
of a fever, a London correspondent wrote to Archbishop Boyle:

> Yesterday I spent my whole time running to the several
> coffee-houses, where, greatly to my satisfaction, it was the
> whole discourse amongst the rankest and most accursed
> presbyterians the great loss that this nation would have in
> the loss of my Lord Ossory.

This letter was written on 24 July 1680; six days later Ossory was
dead.

(3)

Ossory's illness and death came with little warning. A few weeks

118

earlier he had been appointed lieutenant-governor of Tangier, which had come into English possession as part of the queen's dowry and was now under threat of attack by the Moors. At first he had welcomed the appointment, for he was a man of action rather than a politician and had distinguished himself in battle on land as well as at sea: in 1678, when he led the English troops in the Dutch service, his outstanding courage in the battle of Mons had won the praise of the French commander, the Duke of Luxembourg; and King Louis XIV had offered him a high command in the French army. But Ossory's satisfaction with his new appointment soon turned to discontent. He found that the force he was to take with him to Tangier was quite inadequate for its defence; but the king, though warned that this was so, refused to increase it. About this matter Ossory spoke quite openly to John Evelyn, his close friend for thirty years, on 24 July 1680; and Evelyn recorded the matter at some length in his diary. The king's refusal to send a force adequate for the purpose 'touched my lord Ossory deeply, that he should be so little considered as to put him on a business in which he should probably not only lose his reputation, but be charged with all the miscarriage and ill success... he looked on this as too great an indifference in his majesty after all his services, and the merits of his father the Duke of Ormond...'. That very evening Ossory took ill while attending, along with the king and the sheriffs of London, a fish supper in Fishmongers' Hall. Next day his illness turned to a malignant fever, in the course of which 'he raved much of Tangier'; and on 30 July he died.

Ossory's reputation, resting as it did on his personal character rather than on any lasting achievement, did not long survive his death; and his name might have been almost forgotten had he not had the good fortune to be the friend of a great poet.[1] In November 1681 John Dryden published his powerful attack upon Monmouth and Shaftesbury, *Absalom and Achitophel*; and he took the opportunity to commemorate Ossory. Having first paid tribute to Ormond:

> Barzillai, crowned with honour and with years,

he then, at greater length and in more personal terms, commemorates his son:

> His dearest hope, with every grace adorn'd
> By me (so Heav'n will have it) always mourn'd,
> And always honour'd, snatcht in manhood's prime

1. There is a good deal about Ossory in Evelyn's diary; but this was not published until the nineteenth century.

By unequal fates and Providence's crime:
Yet not before the goal of honour won,
All parts fulfill'd of subject and of son;
Swift was the race, but short the time to run.
Oh narrow circle, but of pow'r divine,
Scanted in space, but perfect in thy line!
By sea, by land, thy matchless worth was known;
Arms thy delight, and war was all thy own.

When *Absalom and Achitophel* was published the crisis of the Popish Plot had almost passed; but during the interval Ormond had had to struggle hard to maintain his position against the intrigues of Achitophel and his allies.

(4)

Ormond himself received the news of the death of his eldest and favourite son with outward calm: to one who sympathized with him on his loss he replied that since he could bear the death of his great and good master King Charles I he could bear anything. But in a letter to his sister, Lady Clancarty, he expressed what he really felt: 'I shall never, I think, remember the son I have lost but with anguish'. He did not, however, allow his grief to interfere with his duties; and it was natural that he should look to Arran, now his only surviving son, to take Ossory's place. By the end of October 1680 Arran was in England; and there he remained, in London for the most part, until the spring of 1682. He was a soldier, not a politician; and though he was no stranger to the life of London and of the court he could not exercise the same influence or command the same respect as his more famous elder brother, whose place he was trying to fill. Besides this, his relationship with his father was less close and confidential that Ossory's had been. With Ossory, Ormond had corresponded as with an equal; but in his letters to Arran there is often a note of authority. It is significant, too, that Arran most commonly addressed his father as 'Your Grace', a formality that Ossory had not thought it necessary to observe.

Arran himself certainly did not feel equal to the task that had been imposed upon him. Before he had been many weeks in London he wrote to his father:

I wish that you had an abler man than I am upon the place to
act in these intricate times and affairs, for I wish with all my

heart that I were in some quiet retirement.

Ormond dismissed this complaint as selfish; but Arran took the reproof without showing any resentment; and despite his own distrust of his abilities he achieved some success. Like Ossory, he held an English as well as an Irish peerage and so was able to defend his father in the house of lords. It took him some time, he admitted, to 'overcome the awe of speaking there'; but he did overcome it, and could report to his father that Shaftesbury had not 'ventured to have a fling at you since my being in the house'. This did not mean, however, that Shaftesbury had abandoned his purpose. He and his friends were determined to demonstrate that Ireland as well as England was involved in the Popish Plot; Ormond's success in keeping the country quiet and his failure to provide the kind of evidence they wanted stood in their way; and they were determined to secure his removal from office. As a step in this direction they persuaded the house of lords, on 4 January 1681, to pass a resolution declaring that 'there was and is a dangerous plot in Ireland'. Arran was present on this occasion; and, though he could not prevent the passage of the declaration, he was able to expose the falsity of an assertion, made by one member of the house, to the effect that in Ireland the papists were better armed than the protestants.

When Ormond heard that this declaration had been passed he naturally assumed that it would be followed by a direct attack upon himself, either by impeachment or by an address to the king, asking for his removal. 'An address is a softer way that an impeachment', he wrote to Arran, 'but being commonly in general terms it affords no means of vindication, and in that respect is worse than an impeachment, but since I am not to choose I submit to either as it shall please God to order it'. His fears proved unfounded: on the day this letter was written, 18 January, parliament was dissolved; and though a new parliament met at Oxford on 21 March it was dissolved a week later. The dissolution proved to be a turning-point; and from this time onwards Shaftesbury's influence declined. But the king, though his position was now growing stronger, still felt it necessary to be cautious. Early in April he assured Arran, privately, that he had no thought of removing Ormond from the viceroyalty; but when, later in the month, he wrote to Ormond himself, giving a similar assurance, he sent his letter by a special messenger; and Ormond, equally cautious, delayed his reply for almost three months, so that he could send it by the same messenger on his return to London towards the end of July.

121

By that time the fury aroused by the Popish Plot was visibly declining. Its last victim - Archbishop Plunket of Armagh, whom Ormond had tried in vain to save - was executed at Tyburn on 1 July 1681. Next day Shaftesbury, the ablest of these who had sought to use the plot for their own ends, was committed to the Tower on a charge of high treason; and though for some time popular agitation continued, especially in the city of London, within a few months the king was in a stronger position than at any time since Oates's first revelation of a Popish Plot. Had it not been for Ormond's refusal to be frightened or coerced into dangerously repressive measures the outcome might well have been very different.

Ormond's correspondence during the period of the Popish Plot does not suggest that he allowed himself to be greatly upset by the constant attacks upon his conduct of affairs. He provided Ossory and Arran and others on whose support he could rely with the means of defending him against the charges made by his enemies; but he rarely displayed either anger or anxiety. To be be attacked by 'papists and the worst sort of protestants' was, he told Lord Longford, no new experience for him: 'It has been my lot ever since I came into business, and I believe it will be till I am out of it, and of the world'. It was typical of his attitude that he did not allow either the frequent reports of conspiracy in Ireland or the charges brought against him by his enemies in England to interfere with the routine work of administration. He continued his preparations for a meeting of parliament - a laborious task that he might safely have neglected, for the king later changed his mind and the Irish parliament did not meet again until the reign of James II. He was also much concerned about new arrangements then being made for the management of the Irish revenue. This was a matter to be settled in London; and he showed greater uneasiness over the failure of the authorities there to keep him informed about the progress of their discussions that he ever allowed himself to show over the attacks made upon him by Shaftesbury and his colleagues.

Early in 1682, when the excitement aroused by the Popish Plot had died down, Ormond began to prepare for a visit to England. The future management of the Irish revenue was still being discussed; and he thought that his presence in London might hasten a decision. But he would not have undertaken the journey on this account alone; his main purpose was to arrange a marriage for his grandson and heir, the Earl of Ossory, who was now almost seventeen. During the previous couple of years various matches had been proposed; but only one was still being seriously considered. It had been suggested by Arlington who, as the boy's uncle, had a natural interest in the matter. He had, indeed, a double interest, for the bride he suggested was the daughter of his cousin, Simon Bennet. It must, at first sight, seem strange that Ormond should have taken this suggestion as seriously as he did, for the Bennets were an undistinguished family, far inferior to the Butlers in rank and ancestry. Indeed, on a former occasion, Ormond himself had spoken of them scornfully: 'That lord', he once said of Arlington, 'speaks as if he had been born to a blue riband and forgets Harry Bennet, who was a very little gentleman'. The explanation of his readiness to consider the match lay in the fact that Simon Bennet was a man of great wealth, who could give his daughter a large dowry. Ormond himself admitted this frankly in a letter to Arran:

> I should be glad to have some knowledge of the portion
> before the affair be far engaged in, for besides the portion
> there are few other inducements to make it desirable...
> neither the quality or qualifications of the father and mother
> are great attractions.

But Arran was less willing to overlook difference in rank: when writing to his father on the subject he so far abandoned his normally respectful style as to refer almost contemptuously to 'this plan of marrying your grandson to Bennet's daughter'. Indeed, Arlington seems to have been the only person who showed any enthusiasm about the proposed match; and in February 1682 he induced his cousin to sign an undertaking to agree to it, though the conditions set out were somewhat vaguely worded. It was probably as a result of this undertaking, of which Arlington at once sent him a copy, that Ormond began to prepare for a visit to England.

There was considerable delay before he was ready to set off. He could not, of course, leave Ireland without the king's permission; and about this he had no reason to expect any difficulty. But he wanted to ensure that Arran would be made lord deputy during his absence; and since he felt that he could not himself put such a proposal to the king he asked Arlington to do so. As an inducement, he promised that he would himself bear the cost of Arran's maintenance while he held office, a charge that would normally fall upon the crown. Arlington managed the business successfully; and early in March he assured

Ormond not only that Arran would be appointed deputy but also that the king had approved of the proposed match between Ossory and Simon Bennet's daughter. Arran's journey to Ireland was delayed by the birth of a son, on 16 March; but he arrived in Dublin before the end of April and very shortly afterwards Ormond and his wife took ship for England.

CHAPTER X

Farewell to Ireland

(1)

Ormond and his duchess had an easy passage across the Irish Sea; but the journey from Chester onwards. 'through worse ways than ever were known at this time of the year', was even slower than usual; and it was not until almost a fortnight after their departure that they reached London. Their reception was a clear indication of the change that had taken place in political circumstances. Less than eighteen months earlier Ormond had been threatened with impeachment; now he was given a princely welcome and escorted into the city by twenty-seven coaches and three hundred gentlemen on horseback. The journey and the welcome together proved so exhausting that he found it necessary to rest for two days before going to Windsor to wait upon the king. In a letter to Arran, written after his return to London, he describes his reception at court very briefly: it was, he wrote, 'on all hands as I could wish, and that is enough to say of it'. But even in these few words one can sense his satisfaction in finding, as he did, that he still enjoyed the favour and confidence of the king.

Having paid his respects at court Ormond at once turned his attention to the main purpose of his visit, finding a wife for Ossory. Arlington's proposal of a match with his cousin's daughter came to nothing. In a letter to Arran on 30 May Ormond dismissed it in five words: 'I am quite off with Bennet'. He offered no explanation; but it is probable that he did not consider the amount of the dowry sufficient to compensate for the disparity in rank. It was reported not long afterwards that he had asked for £50,000, which was a great deal more than the highest figure that Arlington, who had promised to 'screw up' his cousin as high as possible, had even hinted at. Ormond lost no time in looking elsewhere. Before he wrote to Arran he had already made an approach to the Duke of Newcastle, who had a daughter of suitable age. But this came to nothing; for the duke professed himself unable to offer any dowry at all. Within a few weeks, however, Ormond's problem was solved for him by the Duke of York. The bride he proposed was his own niece, Anne Hyde, daughter of Laurence, Lord Hyde, who was shortly afterwards made Earl of Rochester. This was a match of which Ormond could heartily approve, not only because the bride was the niece of a royal duke but also because she was the granddaughter of his old friend and colleague, Clarendon. In these circumstances he made no difficulty about accepting a dowry of £15,000; and Arran, who was clearly relieved at having escaped a connection with the Bennets, thought this more than he had a right to expect. Since both parties were satisfied, there was no reason for delay; and on 15 July the marriage took place in the chapel of Burlington House.

When Ormond planned his visit to England he had intended that it should not exceed two months. At the time of Ossory's marriage he had been there almost three; and business connected with the Irish revenue and with the proposal, now revived, for a meeting of the Irish parliament, kept him still longer. But by the end of July he was making preparations for his return, though he did not expect to set out until some weeks later. Reports of smallpox in Dublin had so alarmed him that he proposed to travel via Milford Haven, where he could take ship to Waterford; and he hoped to be back in Ireland early in September. This proved an over-optimistic forecast. On 15 August he received, as he reported to Arran on the same day, 'the king's command to dispose myself for residence here this winter'. But when spring came he still remained in England; and it was not until August 1684 that he at last returned to Ireland.

(2)

In his letter to Arran, Ormond made only brief reference to the king's reasons for requiring him to remain in England:

> ...the reasons he gave and his manner of delivering them were very obliging as they expressed confidence in my integrity and some opinion of my capacity to serve him at a time of difficulty.

The last few words are significant. Though the king's position was now much stronger than it had been a year earlier, it was still a difficult one. Shaftesbury was again at liberty, for the jury had thrown out the charges against him. His influence in London had been weakened by the election of royalist sheriffs in June - a matter in which Ormond had taken an active part - but it remained dangerously strong. He had agents and allies in many parts of the country; and he might still be able to use the popular fear of popery for his own ends. It was natural, then, that the king should wish to have at hand a man of Ormond's high standing and long experience, and one on whose loyalty he could safely depend.

In fact, Shaftesbury proved less dangerous than he appeared. His hopes of raising an insurrection came to nothing; and in November 1682 he fled to Holland, where he died a few weeks later. Throughout the country there was still a good deal of uneasiness about the king's policy and much more at the prospect of a Roman Catholic successor to the throne. But among the discontented politicians there was no one capable of organizing effective opposition to the government; and after the exposure of the Rye House plot[1], in June 1683, the king's authority was more firmly established than at any time since the Restoration. Even so, however, more than another year passed before Ormond, by the king's command, returned to Ireland.

During this extended residence in England Ormond was almost constantly occupied. His time was taken up with attendance on the king, meetings of council, duties at court. 'I seldom know what will become of me in an afternoon', he wrote to Arran in September 1682, 'what betwixt the king's business and the queen's and duchess's divertisements to which I am oftener called than stands with my ease or profit'. Early in the following year the proposal to hold a parliament in Ireland, which had been temporarily abandoned, was once more revived, and this added to his labours: 'I have but few certain hours I can call my own', he wrote in June 1683. He did not grudge time or effort spent in the royal service; but he found that his continued residence in England involved him in so much expense that it greatly reduced his prospects of being able to clear himself of debt and leave an unencumbered estate to his successor. His attendance at court - in London, or at Windsor, Newmarket, Winchester - proved very expensive, not only because he habitually travelled with a large retinue but also because he was expected, as lord steward of the household, to 'keep a table' - that is provide dinner - for the king's guests; and this duty, at least as he performed it, cost a good deal more than the emoluments of the office.

1. A plot to kidnap the King and the Duke of York.

Ormond himself, though concerned about the amount of money he was spending, made no attempt to economize. When, towards the end of 1682, he decided to buy a house in London he chose one of the best in the city, Lord St. Albans' house in St. James's Square. The duchess wrote cheerfully to Arran that his father had made a good bargain, having paid only £9,000 for a house that it had cost over £15,000 to build; but she seemed to forget that he had had to borrow the whole of the purchase price and would now be paying almost as much in interest as he had formerly paid in rent. Ormond's decision to acquire a London residence of his own may perhaps have been influenced by the fact that he had, in November, been made a duke in the peerage of England:[1] Arran, certainly, thought it fitting that an English duke should have a house in England. Ormond himself said little about his promotion, beyond expressing relief that he was not obliged to take his new title from some place in England and would be Duke of Ormond in the English as well as in the Irish peerage.

Though Ormond made no attempt to economize, he was clearly uneasy about the expense to which he was put by his residence in London; and he expressed this uneasiness in a letter to Archbishop Boyle, the lord chancellor of Ireland. Boyle's reply is, for the most part, a conventional blending of sympathy and compliment; but it contains a shrewd though friendly comment that goes to the root of Ormond's financial difficulties: '...Your Grace has been all the days of your life so great and generous in your way of living that you cannot now tell how to abate'.

It was typical of Ormond's inability to 'abate' that shortly after buying Lord St. Alban's house he decided that it must be 'better fitted up than my Lord St. Albans left it'; and he removed his family to Hampstead while the work was in progress. He was, as he admitted himself, unskilful in dealing with figures; and it is doubtful if he ever had more than a very general idea of either his income or his expenditure. But at this time he was seriously uneasy about his position; and in April 1683 he sent for his half-brother, George Mathew, who managed his financial business, 'to come over and see what mischief I have done my private affairs by basset and other

1. There may have been some connection between Ormond's promotion at this time and the death of Lauderdale in August 1682. Lauderdale, a Scot who had been made an English duke at the Restoration, was said to have used his influence to prevent Ormond's being placed on an equality with himself.

expenditure here'.[1] Six months later he was still uncertain about his financial position; but there is nothing to suggest that this uncertainty led him to curtail his expenditure.

(3)

Ormond's residence in England proved in the long run damaging to his health as well as to his fortune. When he arrived in London in the early summer of 1682 he was in his seventy-second year; and, though he was still strong and active, he could not stand up indefinitely to the strain imposed by the kind of life he now had to live. In Ireland his duties as lord lieutenant had certainly been heavy; but there he could himself arrange his hours of work, and he could usually find time for the open-air exercise to which he was accustomed. In England he had not the same freedom. He must follow the court as it moved from one place to another; he must attend meetings of the council, whenever and wherever they were held; and he must be ready to undertake such duties as the king might require of him. Arlington knew him well enough to realize how irksome he must find the restraint he was now under: 'I pity you', he wrote in the autumn of 1682, 'for being tied to the city in this hunting season, whereas in the country you would have found so much pleasure and health'. But for almost two years Ormond stood up well to the strain imposed by late hours, frequent travelling and lack of exercise. Indeed, his gout seemed to trouble him less in England than it had done in Ireland - an improvement that Arran attributed to 'the English air', though some, at least, of the improvement may have been due to pills sent to him from Paris by the Comte de Gramont.[2] But, in the end, the pressure proved too great; and early in 1684 he was more seriously ill than at any time since he had almost died of a fever in 1642. On the morning of Wednesday, 5 March, he was feverish after a restless night; and Thomas Short, one of the most distinguished physicians then practising in London, was sent for. Short bled him and applied a clyster; but

1. Basset is a card game in which success depends much more upon luck than upon skill. Ormond was not an enthusiastic gambler; but card-playing was so much a part of court life that he could not avoid it.
2. Philibert de Gramont - brother of the more famous Antoine, duc de Gramont - had married Ormond's niece, Elizabeth. She was the daughter of his sister, Mary, who had married Sir George Hamilton, fourth son of the first Earl of Abercorn. Elizabeth - 'la belle Hamilton' - had been a famous beauty at the court of Charles II.

next day Ormond was worse rather than better. Short was then joined by three other doctors, including the king's own physician, Sir Charles Scarburgh. They bled Ormond twice, taking ten ounces each time, and after this he was somewhat more at ease; but for another twenty-four hours he remained dangerously ill. Then came a change; and, on Saturday, James Clarke, Ormond's controller of the household, reported joyfully to Arran that the doctors had declared him to be 'in all the probability in the world out of danger'. And after this he improved so rapidly that before the end of the month he himself was able to write to Arran, assuring him of his recovery from what he described, characteristically, as 'a fever the physicians thought dangerous'. But he admitted that he was still weak; and from this time onwards the signs of age became more evident.

Early in April, while Ormond was still convalescent, came the startling news of a fire in Dublin Castle. Between one and two o'clock in the morning of 7 April Arran was awakened by the sound of crackling timbers and had barely time to escape from his bedroom before the fire reached it. He at once gave the alarm; and, though a large part of the building was destroyed, he was able, by blowing up a connecting gallery, to prevent the fire from spreading to the powder tower. Later in the day he sent a report to his father. No one had been killed or seriously hurt; and the king, he wrote, 'has lost nothing except six barrels of powder, and the worst castle in the worst situation in Christendom'. He was afraid, as his later letters show, that he himself might be accused of negligence: 'I long to know how the matter is taken by his Majesty, and the ministers of state, being, I think, justly afraid that in this malicious world, the thing may be so misrepresented as that I may be censured for what I could not help'. But Ormond was able to reassure him: 'Both the king and the Duke of York', he wrote on 19 April, 'have spoken with as much kindness and concern of you upon occasion of the fire as any friend you have'.

At the time of the Castle fire Ormond had been in England for almost two years; and the opposition to royal policy that had been dangerously widespread in the summer of 1682, when the king commanded him to postpone his departure, had long since died down. But in his correspondence during the period there is nothing to suggest that he himself had any desire to hasten his return to Ireland. The truth seems to be that he enjoyed the life of the court; and, though he was certainly concerned about the expense to which he was put, he was reluctant to give it up. Even when, in the early summer of 1684, he at last decided to ask the king's permission to return to Ireland, he still thought that he might postpone his departure to the spring of the following year. But the decision was not left to him. On 17 June he reported to Arran that he had received 'the king's leave, or rather his pleasure, that I should return to my charge'; and he at once began to make preparations for his journey.

The decision that Ormond should return to Ireland without any unnecessary delay had a significance of which he himself was quite unaware. The king, now very much under the influence of the Duke of York, had resolved to make radical changes in the Irish administration; and since Ormond could hardly be expected to co-operate heartily in the policy now to be followed he must be removed from office. It is not unreasonable to assume that he was sent back to Ireland in order that the king might escape the unpleasant task of conveying the notice of his dismissal in an interview, which he could hardly have avoided had Ormond remained at court.

Ormond's departure from London was delayed for several weeks. Since he wished his grandson, the young earl of Ossory, to accompany him to Ireland he had to await his return from Flanders, where he had gone to take part in the siege of Luxemburg; for in the seventeenth century it was almost as usual for a young gentleman of high rank to 'see a campaign' as it was for his successor in the eighteenth century to make the grand tour. When Ossory arrived in London, in mid-July, the duchess, whose health had been declining since the summer of 1683, was seriously ill; and a few days afterwards, on 21 July, she died. Four years later, when he lay on his deathbed, Ormond referred to this day as 'the most melancholy I have ever passed in my life'.

The death of the duchess and her burial in Westminster Abbey delayed Ormond's departure; and it was not until 5 August that he set off from Windsor, together with the Earl and Countess of Ossory. During part of the journey he had the company of Sir Robert Southwell, with whom he was on closer terms than with anyone else outside his immediate family; and to him he spoke openly of the loneliness that had oppressed him since his wife's death. He hoped that the business of governing Ireland would 'divert his melancholy' for a year; but at the end of that period he meant to ask the king's permission to spend the rest of his life in retirement. The journey to Chester took, as was usual on such occasions, a considerable time; and it was not until 19 August that Ormond arrived in Dublin. Once there, he lost no time in settling down to work; and his first major task was to survey the state of the army. Arran, a soldier by profession, had been so careful about its training and equipment, that Ormond could assure the king that he had never known it in such good condition 'in all the time I have had the honour to serve your Majesty and the king your father in the place I am in'. Ormond wrote this cheerful report on 26 October; but at that very time letters were on their way to inform him that he was to be removed from the viceroyalty and replaced by the Earl of Rochester.

(4)

The king's letter informing Ormond that he was to be removed from the viceroyalty was written on 19 October; but for some weeks before this there had been rumours in London of changes about to be made in the Irish administration. Peter Walsh, who seems to have been well informed, wrote to Ormond on 21 September to warn him that something was 'a-brewing... relating mightily to your government and the whole kingdom of Ireland'. This warning appears to have made no impression upon Ormond; and the king's letter, which arrived six weeks later, took him completely by surprise. But he did not allow any element of surprise, much less resentment, to appear in his reply to the king; and he was equally cautious in his letters to the Duke of York and to Rochester, both of whom had written to him about the impending change in the viceroyalty. But in writing to Sir Robert Southwell, a month later, he expressed himself more openly:

> Though I have seen and acted a part in as many, and some
> as desperate revolutions as most men, and thought myself
> as well armed against surprise, yet to such a friend as you
> are, I must own that the king's last resolution concerning
> me and this government, with all the circumstances
> belonging to it, found me unprovided, yet I assure you I
> was and am more out of countenance than sorry.

But even to Southwell, his oldest and most intimate friend, Ormond expressed himself with some restraint. In his letters to Arran, who had now joined his wife and family in England, he made little effort to hide his sense of having been ill-used. He even took the trouble to copy out a letter from the king written during the time of the Popish Plot, thanking him for his services to the crown, and sent it to Arran, advising him to keep this letter by him as a reminder that 'kings have no better memories than other men'. Indeed, if one were to judge his attitude to his recall solely from his letters to Arran one would be strongly inclined to think that there was some truth in a comment attributed to the king that Ormond had 'grown old and peevish'.

If Ormond was, indeed, peevish he had some excuse; for he had good reason to believe that the king had allowed him to return to Ireland as lord lieutenant under the impression that he was to retain the office for some considerable time, when, in fact, his speedy recall had already been decided upon. But he would have accepted his unexpected removal from the viceroyalty more easily had he not believed - rightly, as soon appeared - that his removal was to be the prelude to a radical change of policy in Ireland. That some such change was intended was certainly implied by the reasons given for his recall in the king's letter of 19 October:

> I find it absolutely necessary for my service that very many and almost general alterations should be made in Ireland, both in the civil and military parts of the government; that several persons who were recommended and placed by you, and who were fit to be so at that time, must now be removed, which I think, would be too hard to impose upon you to be the director of. For which reason and others of the like nature, I have resolved to put that government into another hand.

Knowing as he did the trend of royal policy at the time and the strong influence exercised by the Duke of York, Ormond could easily foresee that the effect of these changes would be to replace protestants by Roman Catholics both in the civil administration and in the army; and though he was much more tolerant than the average protestant of his day, he could not look forward without alarm to such a radical change in the distribution of power.

The king, who knew that Ormond would feel himself aggrieved by his unexpected removal from office, did what he could to conciliate him. No time was fixed for the change in the viceroyalty; after he had given up office Ormond was to be free either to remain in Ireland or to come to England; and he was assured that 'in all places and at all times' he would continue to enjoy the royal favour. It was natural that Ormond, foreseeing radical changes in Ireland, should prefer to settle in England; and he asked the king's permission to remain in office until the spring, so that he should not have to make his journey in winter, 'an unfit time for an old man to travel in, or for any man to make provision for his future residence'. To all this the king readily agreed; and Ormond began to consider what preparations he should make for his removal to England.

The first thing he had to settle was the future of the young Earl and Countess of Ossory, who were living with him in Dublin. He thought that they ought to remain in Ireland; and since his successor in office was to be the Earl of Rochester, the Countess's father, this would not mean that they were left without paternal guidance. One reason that Ormond gave for this decision was that Ossory should make himself familiar with the management of the estates that he would one day inherit; but in a letter to Arran he frankly admitted that he did not want to be 'incumbered with the young couple' after his settlement in England. To Rochester he expressed the same view, though in less direct terms: 'I will contribute what I can to their living at ease, but I am resolved if I can to do so myself'. Rochester, though he would have preferred that his daughter and her husband should move to England, acquiesced in Ormond's decision. But the matter was settled otherwise: on 25 January the Countess died of a miscarriage. Ormond, despite his reluctance to be 'incumbered', had been very fond of her and was deeply grieved by her death. It was three days before he could bring himself to write to Rochester, telling him of their 'common and equal loss'; and the plain, unaffected style of his letter conveys an impression of genuine grief.

At the time of Lady Ossory's death the date of Ormond's departure had not yet been fixed; and King Charles had shown no inclination to hasten it. Less than a fortnight later, on 5 February, Charles died; and it was unlikely that his successor, who was eager to inaugurate a new policy in Ireland, would leave Ormond at the head of the government much longer. But when news of the king's death reached Dublin on 10 February Ormond's grief owed little to any thought of how it might affect his own future. Next day it was his duty to proclaim James II; and, to use his own expression, he found it hard to do so with 'the countenance of joy and triumph' appropriate to the occasion. 'I have lost', he wrote to Sir Robert Southwell, 'the best king, the best master, and (if I may be so saucy to say so) the best friend that ever man had'. His unshakeable loyalty to the crown was part of his inheritance; but in his devotion to Charles II there was also a personal affection dating from their close companionship during the years of exile.

Ormond soon felt the difference created by the accession of the new king. Charles had intended that the change of government in Ireland should take place in the manner that he knew Ormond would prefer: he was to retain his rank as lord lieutenant until he came to London, where he would surrender the office into the hands of the king himself. But James was in a hurry to make changes in Ireland; and he would not allow any consideration for Ormond to stand in his way. Before the end of February Rochester, who was to have been Ormond's successor, had, instead, been appointed lord treasurer of England; and Ireland was to be governed by two lords justices, Archbishop Boyle and the Earl of Granard. Ormond was, however, allowed to retain office for some weeks longer, while he prepared for the transfer of his household to England; and it was not until 20 March that he surrendered his authority to the lords justices and started on his journey to London. And in the course of this journey he learned, not from any official communication but from a newsletter that he came upon by chance, that his regiment of horse had been taken from him and given to Richard Talbot. But, though he was no longer lord lieutenant, his reception in London was as splendid as on any previous occasion. A long line of coaches and scores of horsemen accompanied him into the city; and when he reached St. James's Square he was welcomed by a great crowd of cheering citizens. It is not unlikely that many of those who greeted him so warmly were already uneasy about the policy that the new king might follow and saw in Ormond a symbol, and perhaps a champion, of the old alliance between church and crown.

CHAPTER XI

And so to a Grave

*The steps downwards are very natural from a field to a garden, from
a garden to a window, from thence to a bed, and so to a grave.*
(Ormond to Sir Robert Southwell, 18 November 1686)

(1)

Ormond's departure from Dublin in March 1685 marks the effective
end of his long political career. Until his health finally broke down in
the summer of 1687 he continued to attend court and to perform his
duties as lord steward of the household; but he was not in the king's
confidence and he knew no more of his intentions than was evident to
all the world. His rôle in politics now was that of an observer, not a
participant; and the change was the natural result of his unwillingness
to go along with the king's policy on religion. So far as this policy
was concerned Ormond had made his position clear within a few
weeks of his arrival in London. The king had commanded his
courtiers to attend him to Mass on Easter Day (19 April); and Ormond
took his place in the long procession. But at the door of the chapel he,
with a very few others, stopped short and waited outside until the
king reappeared. His action was in strict accordance with his
principles: he would obey the king in all things lawful; but he would
not go a step beyond. It was on the same principle that he voted
against admitting to the Charterhouse, of which he was a governor, a
candidate whom the king had commanded them to receive without
requiring him to take the customary oaths. When it was pointed out
that this would be contrary to the rules as prescribed by act of
parliament, one of the governors, anxious to please the king, asked
impatiently, 'What is that to the purpose?' 'It is very much to the
purpose, I think', replied Ormond at once, 'an act of parliament is not
so slight a thing but it deserves consideration'. This argument carried
the day; and the king's candidate was rejected.

Ormond's refusal to attend Mass and the part he played in rejecting

the king's candidate for admission to the Charterhouse, though of no
great importance in themselves, give a clear indication of his attitude
to one aspect of royal policy in England. But his correspondence
during the period would suggest that he was much more deeply and
more continuously concerned about the policy being followed in
Ireland. Rochester, who was to have been his successor, had instead
been appointed lord treasurer of England; and the Irish government
remained in the hands of lord justices until January 1686, when
Clarendon, Rochester's elder brother, took up office as lord lieutenant.
But both before and after Clarendon's arrival the dominant figure in
the Irish administration was Richard Talbot, who was created Earl of
Tyrconnell in June 1685. He arrived in Dublin very shortly after
Ormond's departure; and though his formal authority was limited to
military affairs he exercised a powerful influence on all branches of
the administration; and no one dared to question his actions, for he
was known to have the full support of the king. Even before his
appointment as lord deputy in February 1687, after Clarendon's
recall, he was the real agent of royal policy in Ireland. He made no
attempt to disguise what that policy was. 'By God, my lord', he
exclaimed to Clarendon, 'these acts of settlement and this new interest
are damned things'; and he was determined that the land settlement of
the 1660s must be reversed and both property and power transferred
from protestants to Roman Catholics.

Ormond, whose correspondents in Ireland kept him informed of
what was happening there, watched the situation with growing alarm
and indignation. He had left Ireland in a more settled and prosperous
condition that it had known for a long time; and now his work was
being undone by a man who had long been his most bitter personal
enemy. He was convinced, not without some justification, that
Tyrconnell, in his re-modelling of the army, had deliberately selected
for dismissal officers whom Ormond himself had appointed; and he
expressed his indignation in strong terms. It was, he wrote, 'the
greatest affront it was in his power safely to put upon me, in the face
of a kingdom I had so long governed and of an army I had so long
commanded'. This was written in October 1685, while Tyrconnell's
work in Ireland was still at an early stage. Less than eighteen months
later Ormond's concern is not about any insult to himself, but about
the state of the country: 'I did not think it probable that without war,
pestilence or famine, Ireland could be brought to the condition it is in,
and to the desolation that threatens it'. To protestants living in

Ireland the situation seemed even more threatening that it did to Ormond viewing it from London; and it was well for his peace of mind that all those about whom he cared most were with him in England.

(2)

Some passages in Ormond's letters during these years suggest that he had meant to return to Ireland and end his days there; but if this had ever been his intention Tyrconnell's policy led him to change his mind. 'I confess I did not soon enough foresee', he wrote to George Mathew in February 1687, 'that it was possible that in this king's or his brother's reign I should be put to seek for a habitation or retreat out of the country where my fortune lies; but it has so far come to pass that I had rather live and die in Carolina than in Ireland'. One may doubt, however, if he would in any case have wished to leave England, where all his surviving children and grandchildren were now settled. It was naturally about Ossory, the heir to his title and estates, that he was most concerned. Though he had been deeply grieved by the death of the countess, he was anxious that Ossory should marry again as soon as possible, for he hoped to see the birth of a great-grandson before he died. It was with this in mind that he gave up any idea of leaving Ossory in Ireland, for it was in England that he must look for a suitable match; and they set off from Dublin together. During the voyage across the Irish Sea Ossory became so ill that he had to be left at Knowsley with his sister, the Countess of Derby, while Ormond continued his journey to London; and before he had gone very far he was overtaken by a messenger with the news that Ossory was sick of the smallpox. But even before he was assured of his grandson's recovery Ormond continued to plan his marriage.

At Northampton he was joined by Sir Robert Southwell, his oldest and most trusted friend; and it was Southwell who suggested a match between Ossory and Lady Mary Somerset, daughter of the Duke of Beaufort. At first sight this must seem a strange alliance to propose to Ormond, for Beaufort was the son of that Earl of Glamorgan who had caused him so much trouble in the 1640s. But Beaufort had renounced his father's faith and turned protestant; and though he supported Cromwell in the 1650s he had later on changed sides and had forwarded the restoration of the monarchy, a service which King Charles had rewarded by making him a duke. Ormond accepted

139

Southwell's suggestion, and all went well. Beaufort readily agreed to the proposed match. Ossory recovered so completely that he was able to take part in the campaign against Monmouth in July.[1] And on 3 August, less than a month after the battle of Sedgemoor, the marriage took place.

At the time of Ossory's marriage Ormond, though now nearing the end of his seventy-fifth year, was still strong and active: a few months earlier, at a dinner attended by the officers of the army on the eve of his departure from Dublin, he had demonstrated the steadiness of his hand by raising a brimfull glass to his mouth without spilling a drop. But from the autumn of 1685 onwards his health began to decline: in September he had a return of the fever from which he had suffered in March 1684 and this was followed by a sharp attack of gout. It was not until the end of October that he was sufficiently recovered to remove to Hampton Court in order, as he told Lord Mountjoy, 'to confirm my health by my usual exercises' - riding and hawking. The improvement did not last; and early in January he was again suffering from gout. Now, however, he was much less concerned about himself than about Arran, his only surviving son, who was slowly and painfully dying of pleurisy. How deeply Ormond was affected is clear from the correspondence of one who attended on the patient: 'The good old gentleman is struck to the very brink of the grave with it, being unable to speak, but with eyes brimfull as his heart'. And after Arran's death, on 25 January, the same correspondent described 'how heavily my lord duke takes the being deprived of this staff of his age, for during the greater part of this time he has never been known to eat and sleep so little, sit so pensive, fetch such deep sighs and look so set and stern'. After Arran's death Ormond became in fact what he had long been in years, an old man; but it was not until eighteen months later that he himself was obliged to recognize, and then reluctantly, that this was indeed so.

It was probably because he felt that he needed a change of scene after Arran's death that Ormond decided to leave London for a time and spend a few weeks in the country. He had a suitable house at his disposal: Clarendon, before his departure for Dublin, had offered him

1. The Duke of Monmouth, an illegitimate son of Charles II, claimed that his parents had been married and that he was the legitimate heir to the crown. He raised an insurrection and was defeated at Sedgemoor.

the use of Cornbury, his seat in Oxfordshire;[1] and Ormond, in return had invited Clarendon to make use of Kilkenny Castle. Early in February Ormond's controller of the household, James Clarke, arrived at Cornbury with a coachload of servants and a wagonload of supplies; and by the middle of the month Ormond himself was in residence and preparing to receive guests. He gives a list of those expected in a letter to Sir Robert Southwell: 'Our young lady and her lord, my Lord of Derby and his wife and, I hope, my Lord of Chesterfield and his daughter will be here this week'. He adds, significantly, that the coachman who drives Ossory and his wife will be strictly charged 'to drive safely and carefully when he meets with rugged steps': Lady Ossory was now with child; and Ormond, looking forward hopefully to the birth of a great-grandson, would take no risks.

It was while he awaited the arrival of his guests that he began to prepare what he described as a 'discourse', setting out the rules of conduct, especially in the choice of friends, that his own experience had taught him. This discourse was intended for the guidance of Ossory, to whom he meant to leave it as a legacy; but, though there is evidence to show that it had been completed, it had disappeared by the early eighteenth century. The letter that was intended to serve as an introduction to it has, however, survived; and it is dated at Cornbury, 16 February 1686. The main theme of this letter is that Ossory should in all circumstances consult with Sir Robert Southwell and be guided by his advice. There was no one in whom Ormond himself had such great confidence; and although the party about to assemble at Cornbury was essentially a family gathering, Ormond's only reason for not including Southwell was that he had been ill and was not yet fit to travel.

James Clarke, whose duty it was to ensure that Ormond and his guests were comfortable, thought Cornbury an inconvenient house and complained that it was 'but poorly furnished' so far as plate and linen were concerned. Ormond, however, liked it very well; and he remained there until April, when he went to Badminton, the Duke of Beaufort's seat in Gloucestershire. By the end of the month he was in London; and there he remained until October, apart from brief visits to Hampton Court and Windsor and, in July, another visit to Badminton. It was from his house in St. James's Square that he wrote

1. There is a contemporary description of Cornbury in *The diary of John Evelyn,* ed. William Bray, ii. 168-9.

joyfully to Clarendon on 24 September:

> My granddaughter Ossory was this morning a little before
> seven o'clock brought to bed of a son. Both she and the
> child are as well, I thank God, as can be expected.

As soon as Thomas, as he was christened after his grandfather - or
Lord Thurles, to give him his courtesy title - was big enough to crawl
or toddle about Ormond was never happier than when in his company.

Ten days after the birth of his great-grandson Ormond, satisfied
that both mother and child were thriving, retired to Cornbury, where
he remained for some weeks; and he was there again in February and
March. Long before this, however, he had decided that he should
have a country house of his own; and he had even sent to Ireland for
hawks and a pack of hounds, so that he might follow his favourite
sports. But he had difficulty in finding a house that suited him: in the
course of twelve months he inspected and rejected at least five. It
was not until March 1687 that he found one that satisfied his
requirements: Kingston Hall (now known as Kingston Lacey), in
Dorset.

It is clear, from a comment he makes in a letter to Sir Robert
Southwell, that Ormond did not regard Kingston Hall as a place
where he might occasionally spend a few weeks when his duties at
court allowed him, but as the home in which he would end his days
when he had finally given up attendance at court. At the time when
this letter was written he was preparing to attend the king on a long
progress through the west; and it is at least doubtful if he would,
when the progress ended, have been willing to retire at once into
private life. The decision was, however, made for him. In August,
before joining the king on his progress, he made a visit to Badminton;
and here he had an attack of gout so serious that it confined him to his
room for a month. The route followed by the king on his progress
included Badminton, both on the outward journey and on his return;
and on each occasion he visited Ormond in his room. James was not
often gracious to those who differed from him; but he was generous
enough to recognize that Ormond's long and unselfish service to the
crown deserved this mark of royal favour.

Ormond never saw either the king or the court again. Almost three
years earlier, shortly after he knew that he was to be removed from
the viceroyalty, he had written to Sir Robert Southwell:

> I was determined the next year to beg his Majesty's leave to

retire for the rest of my time, and to think with less distraction of my approaching dissolution. But it has pleased God (who knows how much I need it) to give me the opportunity sooner; and I hope he will also give me the grace to make use of it.

We need not doubt his sincerity, for Ormond was no hypocrite. But old habits die hard; and, when the time came, he found it difficult to abandon altogether the kind of life to which he had so long been accustomed. Now retirement was forced upon him; and he accepted it without complaint, or any sign of regret. When he was sufficiently recovered to bear the journey he was taken to Kingston Hall; and there he remained, watched over by Lord and Lady Ossory and enjoying the company of his great-grandson, the little Lord Thurles, until his death less than a year later. He was now so weak that he could hardly walk without help; but his mind remained clear to the end: a wish he had more than once expressed that he should not 'outlive his intellectuals' was granted. When Sir Robert Southwell, who had undertaken to write his biography, spent three weeks with him in the spring of 1688 he was as well able as ever to discuss the many important transactions in which he had taken part.[1] This visit probably did him good; for in the early summer he was able to take the air, either in the gardens or in his coach, accompanied by Lady Ossory. By July he was obviously growing weaker; and he himself realized that the end was now near. He prepared for it as calmly as he would have done for any other event that called for courage and confidence. On Saturday, 21 July - the fourth anniversary of his wife's death and for him the saddest day in the year - he arranged with his chaplain to receive the Sacrament the following morning. Later in the day he became doubtful if he should live so long; and it was on the 21st that he made his last Communion, in the presence of Lord and Lady Ossory and his whole household. A few hours later, while his attendants were settling him comfortably in bed, he died peacefully, without even a sigh. A fortnight later he was, as he had wished, buried beside his wife in Westminster Abbey.

(3)

From the age of twenty-five until within a few years of his death

1. Southwell never completed his biography, but the manuscript of what he had written was later used by Thomas Carte.

more than half a century later Ormond was almost continuously engaged in the king's service. His outstanding qualities were courage, patience and, above all, loyalty. It was these qualities that enabled him to maintain the royalist cause in Ireland against greatly superior forces during the 1640s and, a generation later, to keep Ireland quiet during the frenzy of the Popish Plot. He was neither a great statesman nor a great soldier; he cannot be reckoned among the handful of men who may be said to have shaped the course of history; but among those who played a leading part in the political life of the British Isles during the seventeenth century there were few who stuck so consistently to their principles in the face alike of danger and temptation.

Ormond's loyalty to the church was quite as strong as his loyalty to the king. His protestantism was, as we have seen, the result of an accident:[1] it was his father's death in a shipwreck that enabled King James to claim the heir as a ward of the crown and have him brought up as a protestant. Ormond himself referred to this in a letter to Sir Robert Southwell, written at the time of the Popish Plot:

> My father and mother lived and died papists, and bred their children so, and only I, by God's merciful providence, was educated in the true protestant religion, from which I never swerved towards either extreme, not when it was most dangerous to profess it, and most advantageous to quit it.

Ormond's assertion of his constancy was well founded. His loyalty to the church was even stronger than his loyalty to the crown: on one occasion, when he feared that the king might command something contrary to the interests of the church, he declared that in such circumstances he could 'obey only by suffering'. His resolution was never put to the test; but his conduct during the reign of James II suggests that he would have stuck to it.

Despite his strongly held protestantism Ormond was free from the horror of 'popery' then so widespread among protestants. He was too deeply attached to his mother, his brothers and his sisters - all of them Roman Catholics - to speak hardly of the faith by which they lived. His experience during the 1640s made him suspicious of clerical influence in politics. But he believed that loyal subjects, whatever their faith, should be fairly treated: he could not see, he declared on one occasion, why a man's religion should deprive him of his birthright. His own religion as a member of the established church was much

1. Above, page 8.

more than a matter of outwards conformity. The sincerity of his faith appears not only in the prayers and meditations that survive among his private papers, but also, and more convincingly, in his conduct: though the society in which he lived during the restoration period was notoriously licentious, he himself remained throughout life faithful to his marriage vows; and he was one of the very few among Charles II's courtiers who refused to flatter or bribe the king's mistresses. His character had been formed in the 1630s and 1640s; and, just as he continued to the end of his days to wear his hat in the manner that had been fashionable in the reign of Charles I, so he continued to guide his conduct by the principles he had been taught in early life. Macaulay may have exaggerated when he described him as 'the most illustrious of the Cavaliers of the great civil war', but we can safely say that no one was more constantly loyal to the Cavalier principle of loyalty to church and crown.

It is not easy to assess Ormond's place in the history of Ireland. His removal from the viceroyalty in 1685 was followed by a radical change in the Irish administration; and this in turn hastened the revolution in the monarchy that took place within a few months of his death. The Ireland that emerged after the final defeat of James II and his supporters was very different from the Ireland that Ormond had governed in the reign of Charles II: it had entered upon the period of the penal laws and the systematic restriction of its economy in the interests of England. Ormond thus stands at the end of an epoch. The policies he had followed, so far as he was allowed any freedom of action, were abandoned or reversed: and he must be judged by what he attempted rather than by what he accomplished. But there is at least one lasting memorial of his concern for the welfare of his country: it was in his time and under his direction that the transformation of Dublin into the splendid city that it later became had its beginning. And no memorial could be more appropriate: for Ormond himself may fairly be regarded as a prototype of the Anglo-Irish nobility and gentry of the eighteenth century whose good taste made Dublin one of the most distinguished among the smaller capital cities of Europe.

EPILOGUE

At his death Ormond left only three descendants in the male line: James and Charles, the sons of Ossory, and Thomas, the son of James. Thomas died only a few months later; but James and Charles survived into old age. Charles became a soldier and eventually rose to the rank of lieutenant general. In 1693 he was created Earl of Arran in the peerage of Ireland - a title formerly held by his uncle Richard. This was a tribute to his ancestry rather than to his service to the crown, for at that time he was still in his early twenties. Indeed, he never attained any great distinction; and his name survives only as a link in the history of his family.

His elder brother, the second Duke of Ormond, had a much more memorable career. Very soon after his succession to the title Prince William landed at Torbay; and Ormond soon joined him, influenced, perhaps, by the fact that he was related, through his mother, not only to the prince himself but also to several of the senior Dutch officers who had come in his train. At the coronation of William and Mary, in February 1689, he held the important office of lord high constable; and in the following year he was with the king in Ireland and took part in the battle of the Boyne. For more than twenty years thereafter he was continuously engaged in the royal service: he held a succession of military commands and he was twice lord lieutenant of Ireland. Though he showed no outstanding ability, either as soldier or as administrator, he had, like his father before him, a great reputation with the English public. But he lacked Ossory's strength of character. During the last years of Anne's reign he began to waver in his loyalty to the settlement made in 1688-9; and he opened a correspondence with the leading Jacobites, both in England and in France. It is uncertain how far he committed himself; and when Anne died, on 1 August 1714, he was among those who signed the proclamation of George I. But when parliament met in the following year he was threatened with impeachment on a charge of treason; and in August, rather than face his trial, he fled to France. This was taken as evidence of his guilt; and before the end of the month he had been attainted, his English and Scottish titles and honours extinguished and his English estates declared forfeit to the crown.[1] In the following

1. Ormond had the title of Lord Gingwall in the peerage of Scotland.

year an act of the Irish parliament confiscated his Irish lands.

During the insurrection of 1715 Ormond made an unsuccessful attempt to win support for the Jacobite cause in the west of England. But after that he spent the rest of his life in exile and died in Avignon in November 1745. At that time a Jacobite army was marching through the north of England. But six months later, when the insurrection had been finally crushed at Culloden, permission was given for his body to be brought to England; and in May 1746 he was buried beside his grandfather in Westminster Abbey. It was an appropriate place for him to lie. During his long exile he had resisted all inducements to change his faith; and he died, as he had lived, a loyal member of the English church.

Ormond's successor as the head of the Butler family was his brother, the Earl of Arran. Thirty years earlier Arran had already succeeded him in another capacity, The second Duke of Ormond, like the first, had been chancellor of the University of Oxford, having been elected within three days of his grandfather's death. On his attainder in 1715 the office became vacant; the university, where Tory influence was strong, elected his brother in his place; and Arran remained chancellor until his death in 1758. Thus, for a period of almost ninety years - from the election of the first Duke of Ormond in 1669 to Arran's death - the highest office in the university was held in succession by three members of the Butler family.

Arran died childless; and the headship of the family passed to John Butler of Kilcash, great-grandson of the first duke's youngest brother, Walter. John Butler left no son and was succeeded by his cousin Walter Butler, who died in 1783 and was succeeded by his son John, who was M.P. for Kilkenny city. Down to this time it had been assumed that the acts of the British and Irish parliaments in 1715 and 1716 had extinguished the Irish as well as the English titles of the family. John Butler questioned this assumption; and he turned out to be right. The Irish act of 1716, which confiscated Ormond's Irish estates, contained no provision relating to titles of honour, probably because it was assumed, mistakenly, that these had already been extinguished by the English act of the previous year. Succession to the marquessate and dukedom conferred upon the twelfth earl had been confined to the heirs of his body; and these titles had become extinct. But the earldom of Ormond was of much older date; and

John Butler claimed it by virtue of his descent from Walter, the eleventh earl. His claim was allowed by the Irish house of lords; and in 1791 he took his seat as seventeenth Earl of Ormond.

A guide to further reading

There are two biographies of Ormond:

Burghclere, Lady (Winifred Gardner), *Life of James, first Duke of Ormonde* (2 vols., London, 1912).
Carte, Thomas, *Life of James, first Duke of Ormonde* (3 vols., London, 1735-6; Oxford, 6 vols., 1851).

Carte includes a great many letters written by or to Ormond. They occupy the whole of volume III in the edition of 1735-6; but there are some in the other volumes also. He had found these among the papers in Kilkenny Castle, the principal residence of the Butler family, and he transferred a great many of them to England. They are now in the Bodleian Library in Oxford. Much later a considerable part of what remained in Kilkenny Castle was published by the Royal Commission on Historical Manuscripts in ten volumes (1895-1920). The letters contained in these volumes throw a good deal of light on Ormond's character and on his family life.
As well as the biographies mentioned above there is a short but important essay on Ormond ('An illustrious Cavalier') in C. Litton Falkiner, *Essays relating to Ireland* (London, 1909).

The following works provide information about the period in Ireland and in England:
Bagwell, R., *Ireland under the Stuarts* (3 vols., London, 1909-16).
Beckett, J.C., *The making of modern Ireland*, 1603-1923 (London, 1966, 1981), Chapters I - VI.
Clark, G.N., *The later Stuarts* (Oxford, 1940).
Clarke, A., *The Old English in Ireland, 1625-42* (London, 1966).
Coffey, D., *O'Neill and Ormond* (Dublin, 1914).
Davis, Godfrey, *The early Stuarts* (Oxford, 1938).
Foster, R.F., *Modern Ireland, 1600 - 1972* (London, 1988), Part I : The seventeenth century.
Kearney, H.F., *Strafford in Ireland* (Manchester, 1959).
MacCurtain, M., *Tudor and Stuart Ireland* (Dublin, 1972)
Moody, T.W. et al., *A New History of Ireland*, iii (Oxford, 1976) Chapters IX - XII and XVII.

Index

6; goes to France, 46-7; returns to Ireland, makes a new treaty with the Confederates and is defeated by Michael Jones at Rathmines, 47-52; leaves Ireland, visits his family at Caen and then joins Charles II, 57-60; visits England in disguise, 63-6; rejoins the king at Brussels, 68; accompanies Charles on his return to England in May 1660, 74; recovers his estates, 75-6; appointed lord lieutenant, 81-2; foils a plot to seize Dublin Castle, 85-7; his share in the settlement of landed property in Ireland, 87-93; negotiates with the Roman Catholic clergy, 95; his removal from the viceroyalty in February 1669, 96-99; elected chancellor of the university of Oxford, 103; escapes an attempt to kidnap him, 103-4; Ossory accuses Buckingham of involvement in this, 104-5; returns to Ireland, June 1673, 108-9; goes to England for a meeting of parliament in April 1675 and remains there until May 1677, when he returns to Ireland as lord lieutenant, 109-112; his policy during the 'Popish Plot', 115ff; returns to England and seeks a wife for his grandson, Ossory, 123-6; returns to Ireland after the death of the duchess, 131-2; receives notice of his removal from the viceroyalty, 132; receives news of the death of Charles II, 134; goes to London and arranges a match for Ossory, 139-40; his grief at the illness and death of Arran, 140; retires to Kingston Hall, where he dies, 142-3; buried in Westminster Abbey, 143; an assessment of his career and character, 143-5

Butler, James, Earl of Ossory and 2nd

Duke of Ormond; at Oxford University, 114; his marriage to Anne Hyde, 126; takes part in the siege of Luxemburg, 131; death of his wife, 134; marries Lady Mary Somerset, 139; joins William of Orange in 1688, 147; twice lord lieutenant of Ireland, 147; turns Jacobite in 1715, joins in the insurrection and dies in exile, 1745; buried in Westminster Abbey in the following year, 148

Butler, John, Earl of Gowran, 45, 77; marriage and death of, 106-7

Butler, John, 17th Earl of Ormond, 149

Butler, Mary, daughter of 1st Duke of Ormond, marries William, Lord Cavendish, 78

Butler, Richard, Earl of Arran, 45, 77, 93, 94, 106, 111, 120-21, 124, 125, 126, 130, 132, 133, 134; illness and death of, 140

Butler, Theobald, first of the family to settle in Ireland, 3

Butler, Theobald, nephew and son-in-law of Thomas, 10th Earl of Ormond, 1, 2, 6

Butler, Thomas, 7th Earl of Ormond, 4

Butler, Thomas ('Black Tom'), 10th Earl of Ormond, 1, 2, 5-6

Butler, Thomas, Earl of Ossory, eldest son of the 1st Duke of Ormond, imprisoned by Cromwell, 68-9; goes to Holland where he marries, 69, 71; watches over his father's interest at court, 96; in Ireland as lord deputy, 97; his popularity in England, 105-6; made a knight of the Garter, 106; defends his father's policy during the 'Popish Plot', 117-8; his death and Dryden's tribute to him, 118-20

153